The Dawn of Generation Why

Isaiah B. Pickens

An iOPENING ENTERPRISE

Cover illustration: Colin Bootman
Cover design: Emanuel Jenkins

Printed in the United States of America
First printing July 2010

For more information and additional resources, visit www.GenerationWhyMovement.org.

ISBN 145-3630-97X
EAN-13 9781453630976

Contents

Acknowledgments

This book would not have been possible without the support of several people. First I want to thank my family for their constant support, especially my parents, Drs. David and Wanda Pickens. Their encouraging words and initial review of the book helped me tremendously. My brothers, Darius and David Pickens, provided insightful feedback about my ideas.

I am also thankful for the friends and colleagues who supplied immeasurable support and guidance over the past few years. Their feedback on numerous drafts challenged me to dig deeper within myself and search for the right words and ideas. They include Sherri Axelrad, Joshua Bartholomew, Dr. Desiree Byrd, Shakir Cannon-Moye, Danielle Chao, Diana Cheruvil, Sidney Cohen, Marilette De La Cruz, Dr. Christina Gee, Jan Haldipur, Gina Mattivi, Melody Mitchell, Anissa Moody, Christine Lewis, Robin Parker, Rita Sinha, Azizi Seixas, Emily Sachs, Dr. Ryan Watkins, Jason Williams, and Eric Woodard.

I am grateful for the professional support I received from my copyeditor, Liz Sweibel; cover designer, Emanuel Jenkins; and cover illustrator, Colin Bootman. Finally, I want to thank God and my faith for providing the personal strength and perseverance to complete this project.

Introduction

In the November 6, 2005, issue of *USA Today*, Bruce Tulgan, a researcher who studies the lives of young people, was quoted as saying, "unlike the generations that have gone before them, Generation Y has been pampered, nurtured and programmed with a slew of activities since they were toddlers, meaning they are both high-performing and high-maintenance." According to most estimates, Generation Y (Gen Y) includes individuals born between 1980 and 1995. Bruce Tulgan's description of Gen Y has become one of many different voices describing the generation that is moving from the lecture halls of high schools and colleges into the boardrooms and corporate buildings considered sacred by previous generations.

As a member of Gen Y, I have grown fond of the many descriptions, which seem to multiply in number as we become more and more embedded in every part of, well, everything. Initially described as simply an extension of Generation X, "Generation Y" was coined in the Chicago-based magazine *Ad Age* in 1993. As we grow older and become more distinctive as a group, so do the descriptions. Some categorize us as "Echo Boomers" because we are the children of the Baby Boomer generation and represent the largest generation since the baby boom of the 1950s and 60s. Our massive numbers become more and more visible as we graduate from school and enter the workforce to replace retiring Baby Boomers and work alongside Generation X-ers. Our entrance into the workforce has led many to wonder about this new breed of worker who has infiltrated the sanctity of the workplace. Some say that Gen Y is too casual, too concerned with personal life issues, and too in need of constant self-esteem maintenance, while others note that Gen Y is technologically savvy, very connected with one another, and entrepreneurial.

Those who dissect these alleged traits of Gen Y come up with a number of theories that attempt to capture our essence as a generation. Some argue that our parents are responsible for who we are. The lack of attention paid to our parents by our grandparents, due to oversized families and an understood rule that children are not adults' friends, have led many to suggest that our parents made every effort to do the exact opposite of their parents. As opposed to the "Silents" (our grandparents), our parents carefully planned for a family, gave us just about anything we needed to succeed, and told us that we were special and could become anything we wanted. Those who hold this theory believe this created an unshakeable self-confidence in the typical Gen Y-er that manifests itself in every area of life – even when it is not in anyone's best interest. Some believe that our parents reinforced this self-confidence at every possible moment with praise for less-than-amazing performance in every activity we attempted and a general mentality that "everyone is a winner." Some believe this is such a strong contributor to the Gen-Y profile that we should be called the "Trophy Generation" because everyone always received a trophy regardless of their performance and, in many ways, we were our parents' little trophies.

An extension of this theory is that society, in addition to our parents, shifted in our favor during the 1980s and 90s. Laws that favored child protection, better educational standards, and entertainment geared toward creating productive little citizens each produced fundamental changes that, in the eyes of many, significantly influenced us at a critical time in our lives. This societal shift toward a child-friendly environment ramped up as we approached the close of the millennium. Since we were the only group of young people present at the turn of the century, many felt this was such a defining convergence that it should become the chief description of our generation. As a result, William Strauss and Neil Howe took the liberty, in their book *Generations*, to rename Gen Y the "Millennials." With the coining of this name, it appeared that the expectations of our parents who stood for revolution and rebellion in their teenage years, plus societal expectations that a future generation will conquer the vices and obstacles their parents faced, would be fulfilled.

While each of these theories has its distinct qualities, they all come to the same conclusion: the focus is on Generation Y. Whether it is the massive size of our generation, the generally high level of parental support and involvement, or the societal shift in perspective on the value of a child, many older people who observe us believe that we think the world of ourselves – and the world should too. Those who argue this point believe that technology has only made this constant focus on ourselves easier and more "normal." Our tech savvy, coupled with the numerous skills we learned in school and from tons of extracurricular activities, has led many from previous generations to think that we consider it blasphemy if someone speaks ill of us, or worse, ignores us all together. This self-focus has become such a prominent feature of our generation that psychologist Jean Twenge wrote *Generation Me*, a title meant to describe our generation's "most salient" quality. Based on her research, Twenge outlines a new brand of self-indulgence and high expectations that affects Gen Y's mental health, physical well-being, and relationships with others.

While these theories represent the major opinions and research on Gen Y, new voices are constantly adding their ideas. Whether we're called Generation Y, Echo Boomers, Trophy Generation, Millennials, or Generation Me, one description is often missing: ours. The voices of the teenagers and young adults who are the subject of these lively and interesting discussions are often absent from the debate over the very issue that means the most to us – us. Plus, the debate often focuses on a few aspects of who we are as a generation, such as our roles as employees or students, and many times neglect the entirety of the Gen Y experience. Often, these descriptions fail to challenge us to think about what it means to be a member of Gen Y, and instead are attempts to assume responsibility for defining our generation.

While society's assertion of such descriptions may have been met with angry rebellion by our parents and silent acceptance by our grandparents during their teenage and young adult years, it is in our nature to ask this question: *Why?* From as early as I can remember, I was taught to question everything. If something did not make sense then I was to ask questions until it did, or not bother with it. The *Why?* that we asked as children was not meant to be disrespectful (most of the time) and the *Why?* we continue to ask as teenagers and young adults is not meant to belittle those who try to give us answers (some of the time), but is a strategy to understand fully the purpose behind anything that we do. For this reason, it is strange to me that few of the descriptions given by previous generations heed our natural inclination to figure out *Why?*.

    As I set out to write this book, I grappled with who the audience should be. Each time I reflected on older generations' perspectives on our generation, it became harder to ignore my desire to ask: *Why do these perspectives exist?* It is a question that I do not feel alone in asking; many among us are also asking it. The question urges us to search within ourselves and examine what we think about our generation. It became increasingly clear to me that to explore this question meant this book could only be for one group of people: Generation Why.

    Like the generations that preceded us, our generation is comprised of people from every possible background. The sheer size of our generation translates into an even greater number of people who are male, female, black, white, Hispanic, Asian, rich, poor, middle class, and so on, indefinitely. This diversity adds to the richness of our experiences as young people in our respective work places, schools, and communities. Regardless of background, each member of Generation Why is attempting to navigate a world with this persistent question: *Why?* It is a question that inspires us to seek meaning and purpose in every aspect of our lives. While our search for the answer to this question binds us, I wrote this book for members of Generation Why who are currently in college and young adults who recently graduated.

After figuring out my audience, I had to figure out what this book would be about. I toyed with many different ideas. Generation Why's journey toward understanding *Why?* is so rich with different experiences. I wondered if I should write about the dread of classes and school that is only countered by the fact that we can meet cool people who will hopefully become close friends for life. I debated whether entering the workforce should be the focus of this book since so many of us are making that transition. I thought maybe I should do a literary version of Will Smith's 90s hit *Parent's Just Don't Understand*, and write about the evolving relationships with our parents as we become older and transition into adulthood. All these perspectives were tempting but do not adequately hit on our description of our own generation.

Then the purpose became clear: to ask the questions of Generation Why that generations before us have asked themselves during young adulthood, but in our unique historical context. These questions are no less important than they were for our parents or grandparents, but sometimes easy to over-look. Why are we the way that we are? Why do we go to school and work? Why are we here on this Earth? Each of us grapples with these questions as young adults. Yet *Why?* is a deeply complex question that, by itself, may not get us the answers we need. We need to ask additional questions.

To spark such questions, the first three chapters and interludes of this book prompt self-reflection. The last three chapters and interludes challenge us to think about how our viewpoints and actions affect others. The chapters deal with some complex topics and highlight some interesting people. The interludes act as breaks between chapters that also provide a creative foreshadowing of the chapter to come. While each chapter's questions may initially appear simple, they have the potential to spark profound answers.

It is beyond the scope of this book to examine any one topic or person in depth. The bibliography offers ways to get more information. The reader's guide, also in the back of the book, offers questions and activities for readers to explore the issues raised more deeply, either on their own or with a group. Altogether, this book is a companion on our personal journeys as members of Generation Why. With that said, I invite you to take a trip with me as our generation tries to figure out its defining question: *Why?*

Prelude:
Conditioned

I can't escape this condition,
Of being conditioned.
The harder I try to rethink my ways,
The more society tells me to remain the same.
The TV, newspaper and radio
Constantly show me that the truth is elusive.
The more I try to know,
The more people tell me to stop being intrusive.

He seems nice,
But he's also white.
He'll probably try to get over not once,
But twice.
She looks smart,
But her skin is awfully dark.
Hmmm, maybe she's part...
White after Labor Day?
They certainly are not from around this way,
'Cause they should afford a better outfit and need to pay...
Attention sir, can you please step to the side?!?!
Remove your shoes and that sheet on your head you call
religious pride!
Ha, you think what I'm thinking is something to hide?
These terrorists make me want to *Sikh* genocide.

I can't escape this condition,
Of being conditioned.
It's our society's favorite addiction.
Having politicians and statisticians
Making all types of policies and predictions,
To perpetuate these ideas and beliefs
Which are many times no more than fiction.
But maybe if we make an effort to acknowledge our
predisposition,
It will put each of us in a position
To make a better decision

About how we help build the world our unborn children envision.
Because if we truly listen to our intuition,
We realize that **just** treatment of all is simply a form of submission
To our greatest earthly mission
To ELEVATE the human condition.

Chapter 1:
Who Are You?

"What lies behind us and what lies before us are tiny matters
compared to what lies within us."

~ Ralph Waldo Emerson

Who are you? What defines you? Are you the titles you
accumulate over the years? Are you the people you choose to
associate with? Are you your religious beliefs? Is the answer
none of the above? The process of defining ourselves is as old
as the VCR, maybe even older. Philosophers, psychologists,
musicians, sociologists, politicians, filmmakers, and everyone
else under the sun have attempted to answer the age-old question *Who am I?*. Greek philosopher Thales laid the
philosophical groundwork for Socrates yet found the most difficult quest in life "to know yourself." Psychologist Erik
Erikson built his career around exploring the question *Who
am I?* by outlining the progression of identity over the lifespan.
Spiritual teacher Eckhart Tolle suggests that truly defining
one's self is beyond words. Many great thinkers have tried to
tackle this question and provide answers for the masses, but
repeated attempts reveal that the answer to this question is
often the result of a deeply personal journey that profoundly
affects every aspect of our lives.

I remember the first time I was asked the question *Who
are you?* I was no older than sixteen. I quickly spouted answers that I thought perfectly defined me: "I am smart. I am

fun. I am ambitious." While these responses touched on who I am, somewhere inside of me I felt they only scratched the surface. They did not fully capture who I am at my core. As I reflect, that's a difficult question to answer at sixteen years old. Even now I wonder, *Is this a question I can fully answer as a young adult?* Understanding who I am is one of the toughest challenges I face on a daily basis. Exploring who I am often leads down roads that are as uncomfortable as they are confusing. A step in one direction brings me face to face with society's expectations of me as a young adult. A step in the other direction involves a direct encounter with the perceptions and opinions of friends, family, and others. Finally, a step straight ahead initiates a head-on collision with the most difficult set of expectations: my own. Each step I take to discover who I am enlivens more questions: *Who do others think I am? Who am I supposed to be? Who do I want to be?*

While these questions prompt personal reflection, it is the universality of the journey to answer the question *Who am I?* that is especially intriguing. As each of us strives to gain clarity about who we are as individuals, our parents and grandparents observe us and nostalgically remember the journey that led to their personal self-awakenings. With each step we take as young adults, they see a part of themselves fighting parents' rules, challenging societal norms, and standing in front of the mirror wondering who is staring back. Their road to self-discovery during young adulthood, like those before them, was often a struggle to close the gap between pervasive

4

expectations and the reality of who they truly were. This universal experience and its encounters with the expectations of society, friends and family, and ourselves lead to this question: *How do the expectations our generation faces affect the journey to discover who we are as individuals and as a generation?*

Expecting the Unexpected

As I reclined in the theater with a bucket of popcorn and prepared for the thrill of *Saw* 79 (I lost count after *Saw* 5), I realized that I arrived well before the movie start time and had the chance to watch a few commercials before the previews. First the advertisements for snacks appeared, then came the department store commercials promoting holiday shopping. Finally, I received a crash course on patriotism and job preparation with an inspiring Marines commercial. Commercial after commercial blared messages urging me to buy this, to try that, and not to miss a once-in-a-lifetime opportunity. As I stuffed another handful of popcorn into my mouth, I could not help but wonder: *Can I escape this condition of being conditioned?*

Put another way, do the expectations faced by young adults today bind each of us to a predestined identity? Scholars suggest that identity is as strongly tied to personality as it is to the environment that begins to mold a person the moment he or she leaves the mother's belly. An even more interesting idea is that the historical context an individual is born into molds the person more than anything else. In other words, the historical events, trends, and popular culture that define a generation may have a significant role in defining the individual. History shows that the Great Depression molded a generation's views on money and the importance of discipline, while the growing awareness of social injustice and the importance of individualism during the 1960s shaped the values of a generation that promoted activism and free love. While these particular historical events were not the sole basis for how young adults defined themselves individually or collectively, they provided the context for young people of those generations to discover themselves and begin answering the question *Who am I?*.

In the novel *Fight Club*, author Chuck Palahniuk asks, "If you wake up in a different time, in a different place, could you wake up as a different person?" I pose a similar question: *If you wake up in **this** time, in **this** place, what person do you wake up as?* Often, I feel that we are not given enough time to reflect on this question. Instead, we are given more than enough ways to provide answers immediately.

Today, we have more tools to express the depths of our individuality than at any time in history. We can share ourselves with the world and get feedback 24/7. Blogs, profile pages, personal Web sites, and hundreds of other outlets for self-expression are simply running thoughts about who the writer is, what he or she thinks, and how he or she relates to the world. Sometimes people post the most boring, non-eventful activities, because the world must hear the melodic song of self-expression. (I only know this because I can be a status-stalker sometimes; yes, I know I'm the only one.)

Yet with all these tools for self-expression, I often feel so overloaded that I rarely have the energy (or desire) to think about who I am. I am constantly bombarded with messages from friends, family, media, and the world around me about what I should do, think, or feel. In fact, it takes intentional effort for me to understand myself apart from all these well-meaning definers. How does being a part of this generation define who we are as individuals and collectively? How do the trends of today, the messages from others, and unprecedented access to tools for self-expression influence what I think of myself? These are questions I constantly grapple with, and I often find more questions than answers.

I often think back to my experiences in school. I remember my first day in high school —a mixture of fear and excitement at the prospect of attending a new school. My head was spinning from trying to listen to the teacher talk, while fighting off nervousness about not knowing anyone. After a couple of days, a kid who was also new approached me and asked if I wanted to be friends. I figured *why not?* because I didn't know anyone else. I hung out with him for a couple of weeks, and two or three others joined us. After a few months, my friends and I had a regular hang-out spot, swapped stories about classmates, and talked about what we were doing together for the weekend. By midyear, everyone in school knew us as a group, and my friends and I assumed our designated position in the social hierarchy. As in most schools, the hierarchy had the cool kids at the top, who seemed to gain adulation from the masses with the least bit of effort, and the unpopular kids who suffered through teasing and occasional wedgies at the bottom. I fell somewhere in the middle of the school pecking order with other students who just wanted to remain under the radar and avoid unnecessary embarrassment (especially wedgies). While this whole process was mostly about finding somewhere to belong, it may also shed light on the question *Who am I?*

After the dust settled and I had my group of friends, I often wondered what led to these people becoming my friends. How did the guy who gave someone a piece of his mind at any moment become the friend of a relatively mild-mannered boy who was taught always to respect authority? Why did the girl who seemed exceedingly reserved and barely spoke befriend the person who loved to get around and meet new people? What attracted me to these people, and vice versa? This final question gave me an inkling of how my friends may provide a gateway for me to understand myself. *What are the characteristics of the people who occupy most of my personal time? Do any of those characteristics seem familiar?*

If we honestly examine the five people who occupy most of our time and compile their traits, likes, dislikes, and general characteristics, we likely have an accurate reflection of ourselves. The people I spend most of my waking hours with or talking to have several qualities I like. In fact, they probably have something that I see in myself or at least would like to see in myself. On a journey toward self-understanding, it is usually easier to look at the qualities and characteristics of others than to look inwardly at our own character strengths and weaknesses. The people we choose to bring into our inner circles often reflect us in some way.

While it is great that friends can provide insight into some personal characteristics, how does that information shed light on our chief concern, *Who am I?* A reflection is a good starting point for digging deeper, but how do we delve to the core from here? At this point I began to think about the school that gave me the opportunity to meet my friends. Then I thought of the music, movies, and television shows that gave my friends and me something to talk about. Then my mind began to imagine the parents who tried to raise kids that would pick "good" friends. My thoughts began to spark ideas about how this web of friends, family, and society could guide me closer to understanding myself.

When asking *Who am I?* it is hard not to think of our parents. Whether or not our parents were actively involved in our lives and whether or not they represented the type of people we should not become, they taught us right from wrong before we were able to make a choice. I remember when my parents restricted me from watching certain shows on television or forbade me from going to a party with my friends. With each new rule and parental "suggestion," my parents shaped my values regardless of whether I agreed. As I grew older and began making some decisions independent of my parents, I realized that some of my parents' values just did not work for me. *I have to be home by what time? I don't think so.* Or, *you don't want me to date who? Why not?* The back and forth between my parents and me eventually turned into arguments.

Through these arguments I came to see how my parents, along with many others, tried to influence me by becoming small insects called *Should-Bees*. While Should-Bees may initially sound a little childish, the underlying concept provides insight into the role others play in shaping who we are. Should-Bees are people who buzz around our lives and tell us who we should be or ought to do. Should-Bees come in all shapes and sizes. Sometimes the mother bee or father bee "strongly recommends" that we date a certain person. Sometimes the teacher and professor Should-Bees direct us toward a particular career path. Sometimes the friend Should-Bees tell us that if we really want to impress that special person we should _____. (Fill in the blank with whatever crazy thing your friends have suggested lately.) While the Should-Bees may have good intentions, their goal is to shift our perspective to see the world as they think we should (i.e., the way they do) and not necessarily as *we do*. Over time, these Should-Bees can cloud our personal ideas and beliefs with their ideas and beliefs.

How do we untangle the two? The first step is to know that some of the ideas and beliefs we've adopted may not really

be *our* ideas and beliefs. When others have buzzed arou. ˉ
our whole lives, it can become difficult to hear the differen.
between the buzz and our own voice.

I remember when I first began to question how much I
agreed with what my parents taught me as a child. It was
when I had my first drink. In high school my friends and I always hung together, except when it came time to party. My
parents believed that unsupervised parties for teenagers were
not even an option. Then college came and the party scene became a bit more familiar. During my entire freshman year, I
partied but refused to drink. Even though no one was of legal
age, everyone was drinking; at least that's how it seemed. The
parties began to wear on me. Having a drink became more
and more appealing. I mulled over why I did not drink. No
matter how hard I tried, I could not think of a better explanation than my parents told me I shouldn't. By the end of the
year, my friends did not even ask me whether I wanted a drink.
They knew the answer was a quick "No."

Yet, my curiosity was high and it won out the last day of
freshman year. As usual, my friends were in the dorm pre-
gaming. I met up with them soon after they started. It was
one of those beautiful spring nights where the energy in the air
matched the vibrancy of a newly awakened season. Everyone
was in the mood to party hard and wake up late. They were just
about to wrap up with the last drink when I said softly, "Fix me
one." My friend came closer, looked at me curiously, and said
"What did you say?". I sheepishly smiled and said, "Fix me

ne." The celebration that followed my first drink was unexpected, but made for a fun night. We all staggered out into a couple of random parties and made some new friends, reconnected with some old ones, and hoped no pictures landed online. After waking up the next morning with a serious hangover, I reflected on my decision to break from my parents and make a personal decision. I experienced the buzz from a drink and the subsequent throbbing headache that came from too many. Did I need to experience it to figure out what I personally believed? No, I did not. However, I did have to ask whether the beliefs I held were based on what I *believed* or what I thought I *should* believe.

This was one of my first experiences reflecting on what I was taught and making a conscious decision to follow a different path. Am I implying that challenging every suggestion from others is the best way to untangle personal beliefs from others' beliefs? Not at all; many times others have valuable knowledge that can help avoid some bad situations. Today I drink occasionally. None of the several reasons that led to this personal decision are someone else's. The reasons are my personal beliefs, and truly reflect who I *am* and not who I *should* be.

To clarify my personal beliefs, I've tried to complete the statement *I believe* _____ for as many topics as I could. I believe that it is important to eat three meals a day. I believe it is my right to skip class. I believe that chickens should be able to fly like every other bird. (I believe random things sometimes.) The list was at first harmless, but as I continued I was forced to think about some tougher issues. *Do I believe I should tell my boyfriend or girlfriend I cheated? If I know it is impossible to finish this paper by morning, is it OK to use an old paper from another class or "borrow" a paper from a friend? I don't want to smoke this, but is it really that big a deal?* As I grew older and became further removed from what my parents taught me, these questions became more frequent and more difficult to answer. To explore the question *Who am I?* adequately, I had to search beyond who surrounded me and delve into what lived within me.

Digging Deeper

It is universally accepted that humans are complex. Looking at movies and television shows that depict characters with so many virtues and vices embodied in one person is sometimes mind-boggling. As opposed to the caricatures of good and evil that our parents' and grandparents' generations had touted to them on television – anything from being a good worker to the evil embodied by anyone who drives fast cars – our generation is presented with a more nuanced view of the human experience. I am reminded of a *Saturday Night Live* sketch that re-created a commercial from the 1950s. Timmy liked Lucy, but Lucy knew that she should wait to have "fun" until she was married. Lucy's parents told her the story of the birds and the bees, but Lucy decided to have fun anyway. By the next scene, Timmy lay dead in the bed beside a tearful, pregnant Lucy as her parents wagged their fingers in the doorway and shouted "I told you not to kiss him."

Even though some of us may not morally agree with having fun before marriage, our generation knows that there are forms of protection that make it unlikely that anyone dies right after a night with Lucy. Nor is a person disdained by our generation if he or she has fun before marriage – even if that fun happens with a person of the same sex. This change in thinking reflects a general shift in our generation when it comes to judging the individual.

What does this shift mean? It bodes well for fostering tolerance. More than any other generation, we possess a fundamental respect for the person irrespective of race, gender, religion, sexual orientation, or ethnic or cultural background. While this is promising, the many possibilities for who we can be may become cumbersome. We have many shoes to fill as young adults today. We are sons and daughters, students, girlfriends and boyfriends, after-school and collegiate athletes, friends, part-time workers, entrepreneurs, brothers and sisters, volunteers, social activists, or church, mosque, or synagogue members; the list continues indefinitely. Each of these roles speaks to an aspect of our complex identities, but are we the sum of our roles? Like my descriptions of myself at the beginning of the chapter, it feels that each of these roles is merely a superficial indicator of who I am at my core. However, the expectation to fulfill many of these roles simultaneously represents a fundamental shift in what others expect of us and what we expect from ourselves.

I remember conversations with my parents about expectations others had for them as they transitioned into young adulthood. My mother said that getting a good stable job and having a family summed up the expectations of her day. Today we want to graduate college, then work a nine-to-five job for a couple of years in order to live young and free with a little extra cash in our pockets. Plus, many of us are so fed up with school by the time we graduate, we'll do just about anything not to go back. We may decide to travel a year or two in order to see the world and learn more about ourselves. During this time we meet different people, but don't concern ourselves with finding a mate. We can do that after we get all the fun out of our system. By the time we are ready to settle down, we want to have created a multimillion-dollar empire that will allow us to retire in the next ten years. Then we can relive our twenties, but with our mates and loads of money.

Maybe this is just my fantasy and maybe it does not describe every Gen Y-er word for word, but it is clear that our generation has different expectations of ourselves than any generation that preceded us. Our generation strives for more out of life at an earlier age than any prior generation. Whether "more" means material wealth or simply life experiences such as travelling the world or starting a business, we often expect to achieve more *now* rather than *later*. In her book *Generation Me,* psychologist Jean Twenge examined expectations among members of our generation and reached the same conclusion. She believes that many of our generation expect much more than we will actually achieve and that will lead to many dissatisfied people.

Are our expectations reasonable? I would like to believe they are, but it is for each of us to decide whether our individual expectations and goals are realistic given our plans to achieve them. What is more interesting, and more relevant to our question, is how we develop these expectations and how they manifest within our generation as opposed to previous generations. Remember in school when a new pair of sneakers arrived in stores? Everyone needed to have those sneakers. If someone didn't get the sneakers, then he or she at least needed to wear the newest clothes. If not, then a nice accessory like earrings, a necklace, or a watch could make up for not having the newest shoes. Everyone *needed* something to ward against the dreaded death knell in any high school reputation: teasing. Kids pleaded with parents to buy "this" or just let them have "that" because all the other kids would think they were cool. It was understood that the cool kids *needed* to meet certain expectations and the way they dressed definitely represented a significant part of the qualification process.

Where did these expectations originate? Did they come from other kids? What we all do to get a sense of what is expected in any situation is compare our personal situations to the situations of others. I like to call it the *Comparison Bug*. Unlike the Should-Bees that buzz around us, the Comparison

16

Bug emanates from within each of us. It is always bugging people; plus, it's contagious. If I see someone compare himself to someone else, then guess who starts drawing comparisons with everyone around? I do. There is nothing particularly wrong with comparing ourselves to others. It builds motivation to strive for more while hopefully accruing gratefulness for what we already possess. It becomes problematic when comparisons lead to negative feelings and stress about our personal identities. The insecurity of not wanting to go to a friend's party because others will whisper unflattering words about me, the heartbreak of not feeling attractive enough in front of the person I really want to take a second look at me, or the sadness that comes from not fitting in are each examples of negative feelings that can arise from the Comparison Bug.

With each comparison there is a certain expectation, and we often feel compelled to evaluate whether we are meeting it. This Comparison Bug is not a new disease that hit our generation and skipped our parents and grandparents. Most people have a crazy uncle in the family who tells a million stories and a couple of those stories end with "but I showed them." That ending means that people expected something from him and he gladly gave them the opposite. What is different about our generation is *to whom* we compare ourselves. Yes, our parents had television and movie stars to follow, but were they constantly exposed to the lives of these stars? There is one word that has completely revolutionized how the Comparison Bug operates: technology. Imagine a reality show for

Elvis Presley or visiting the crib of the Beatles. Previous generations had limited access to celebrities, so our parents and grandparents had few ways to compare their lives with celebrities' lives. Today, on the other hand, there is unlimited access to most anyone's life. If I want to know how many Bentleys a celebrity has, I can just watch *True Hollywood* on television. I can listen to music and hear how much and how many of everything today's celebrities have. Finally, I can always google a celebrity. Our generation created a verb! Whoever heard of googling someone twenty years ago? Each new story on our favorite celebrities provides an opportunity for the media to fuel an image of perfection that each of us *should* aspire to.

Unfortunately, this Comparison Bug is not satisfied with assessing distant celebrities, but would like to hit a little closer to home by sparking comparisons with more familiar faces. We see each other in dorms, at work, around the neighborhood, and when we go out. All of these provide the opportunity to compare who I am and what I have to others. Again, nothing is wrong with this in itself, but if it leads to expecting something from myself that I cannot deliver, then serious personal frustration will soon ensue. Many of our parents and grandparents faced these same challenges and managed to build fulfilling lives and strong families. However, our generation's Comparison Bug is a bit stronger for the same reason that we have more access to celebrities: technology. Unlike our parents' generation, we have the privilege of broadcasting ourselves to the world and seeing into the lives of everyone else with profile pages, self-made videos online, and constant status updates on cell phones, online blogs, and home pages. With this privilege come opportunities to raise expectations for our appearance, career choice, and general lifestyle.

Taken together, both Comparison Bugs and Should-Bees potentially play a significant role in how we each answer the question *Who am I?* More expectations force us to expand how we think about ourselves as individuals. Each such expansion adds pressure to meet both personal expectations and the expectations of others. This pressure may give the most insight into who I am. Like the beauty revealed from a natural diamond formed in the direst of conditions, the key to unveiling the inner essence of who I am may lie in how I deal with the pressure. Thus this question arises: *How do we as individuals and as a generation handle the pressure?*

Hidden Treasure

In our relatively few years on Earth, every young adult has faced (and continues to face) the pressure of expectations. Some encounter the pressure to stay motivated for a job that is not inherently motivating. Others must overcome the pressure to complete a school track that does not remotely match how they envision spending their time. Still others experience pressure to meet a mate, make money, or simply become completely independent from parents. Each single pressure is further intensified by the multiple expectations faced by young adults of our generation. Our reactions to pressure can range from strategic planning to overcome challenges to mental and emotional breakdown. Our different reactions often reflect whether we use the style of the *Whatevers*, *Knows*, or *Nonstoppers* to deal with the pressure.

The Whatevers take a hands-off approach to meeting expectations by not acknowledging the pressure. When confronted about not taking care of household duties or challenged to work harder on the job, their response is "Whatever." It is as if they are unaffected by expectations, but they are actually avoiding the pressure. The Knows, on the other hand, add expectations, with the goal of proving they are more than capable of conquering the pressure. Call it confidence, swagger, arrogance, entitlement, or simply an assured sense of self, but it oozes from many people in our generation. The young employee who believes he should have the same benefits as a senior employee because he thinks *I do just as much as the top executives* or the graduate student who plans to start her small business in the next couple of months because *a nine to five is just not cool* are often Knows. The Knows deal with pressure by creating the appearance that they meet each expectation, regardless of its veracity. Finally, the Nonstoppers face the pressure directly with an ever-present anxiety about whether they did enough to meet expectations. Adding a couple of extra hours to the work schedule, immediately identifying flaws of completed projects, and continuously analyzing ongoing tasks are just a few of the characteristics of Nonstoppers. While the level of anxiety can range from just enough stress for motivation to barely moving without having a panic

20

attack, the result is often met expectations with little relief from the pressure. The qualities that characterize each style may be advantageous in some situations, while detrimental in others.

Collectively, these three styles can empower an individual to overcome the pressure or can cause the individual to succumb to the enormous strain of expectations. However, the potential for pressure relief or expectation exacerbation is unlocked by what lies beneath these styles. If a person values integrity and wants to complete a work assignment at any cost, the Nonstopper's style is effective. If another person believes that quality of life supersedes any work assignment, he or she will respond with "whatever" when pressed to take on extra work. If still another person prefers wealth at a young age, he or she assumes the style of the Knows and accepts any work assignment despite its negative impact on a social life. Undergirding each of these approaches are values that take priority on the *life agenda*. The life agenda is simply a list of what is important to an individual. The response to pressure reveals a person's values and answers *Who am I?*

The difficulty with reaching the core of who I am is that so much keeps it covered. One solution exists: dig! I have to dig past the buzz of the Should-Bees. Then I must empty myself of the dozens, hundreds, or thousands of Comparison Bugs within me. As I get closer to the core, the pressure of the Should-Bees and Comparison Bugs feels overwhelming, but with each shovelful, I dig out just enough to get a peak at someone I never met: me. Digging is difficult because it forces me to ask some tough questions while facing intense pressure to decide what items take priority on my life agenda. It takes personal initiative to pick up the shovel of self-reflection and dig deep enough to reach the core of who I am. Yet it may be the only way to experience true personal freedom.

In his classic novel *Invisible Man*, Ralph Ellison describes the story of a young man who is struggling to figure out his place in the world. At first the young man believes that school and education are his keys to understanding himself. When these fail, he looks to a job. As the story progresses, the character (who is never given a name) gets into a horrible accident and finds himself strapped to a hospital bed. He is trapped. When he regains consciousness, medical staff asks him simple questions like *What is your name?* and *Who is your mother?*. No matter how hard he tries, he cannot answer these questions. Then the character has an epiphany and says to himself, *When I discover who I am, then I'll be free.* This one statement sets events in motion that help him figure out who he is and free him from the hospital. In a way, don't we each become free when we discover who we are? We are freed from the expectations people have of us, the feelings of insecurity we may have about ourselves, and, most importantly, from the pressure that clouds the values that determine priorities on our life agenda.

When I started college, I had no clue who I was or who I wanted to be. I figured that college was the time to try different versions of myself. I tried to become the single-minded bookworm whose sole goal was to achieve, achieve, achieve. I tried being the cool athlete who dated as many women as my Rolodex could fit. I explored the ascetic life and held self-restraint and social semi-isolation as guiding moral principles. With each new version of me, I felt myself drifting further away from the deep questions. The irony of my search to understand myself was that each moment I focused on one small aspect of my identity, I neglected who I am in my entirety. I failed to notice the student who saw schoolwork as a path to learning skills that help people and eventually will connect, not disconnect, him with others. I overlooked the guy who sincerely wanted to get to know a person as a friend so that a special bond could develop, as opposed to a quick moment of self-gratification. I denied the young man whose vulnerable emotional interior would only strengthen if he shed his hard-nose exterior. I forsook opportunity after opportunity to free myself from the subjective opinions and limited perceptions that bound me. I denied myself the chance to embrace all of me. The moment I began to ask myself the honest questions that dug deep was the moment I realized that the hidden treasure was more than discovering who I am and knowing what is on my life agenda.

Our life agenda items range from getting through the day and finishing classes to finding our soul mates. Yet in part, each agenda item is an attempt to answer *Who am I?*. There is an unrelenting drive within each of us to figure out who we are because at our core there is something that whispers, *This is the only way to know what you can give the world.* If we don't know and embrace our strengths, weaknesses, likes, dislikes, and beliefs – if we don't know and embrace ourselves – then how do we know what we can offer the world? We all want to do something that people remember. We each want to achieve something that shouts to the world, "I was here. I meant something!" Thoroughly exploring the question *Who am I?* may be the first step to getting this done and leaving a mark on the world as individuals and as a generation. It may be the first step to understanding our purpose here on Earth, the true hidden treasure. We have plenty of tools to show who *I* am, but we take far less time to reflect on how *I* came to be and to separate *I* from everything else. Have we asked ourselves the right questions so that we can dig past whatever is covering up the answers? Novelist Richard Grant summarizes the importance of answering the question *Who am I?* by poignantly stating "the value of identity of course is that so often with it comes purpose." I have a feeling that this is not just my purpose or your purpose, but our purpose – a generation's purpose.

Interlude:
The Wake of Potential

We are here to celebrate the life of one of God's greatest children. Born August 4, 1924, Potential Smith was the son of Action and Faith Smith. As a young child, Potential was a precocious youngster with an inquisitive spirit and unwavering desire to learn, learn, and learn some more. By age four he had already begun first grade and even tutored kids in kindergarten ... on what I don't know, but that's Potential. He had a fondness for his mother, Faith, and would spend hours listening to her sing and watching her paint. Faith speaks of singing to Potential about their family's blessings and painting the songs she sung. Her melodious tone would feed Potential visions of things which no man had seen or heard. To Faith's surprise, Potential became very fond of writing. His stories seemed to have a consistent theme of people transforming into something better and more beautiful than they were before. Faith remembers one story in particular that he told her on his tenth birthday. It was about a young boy who became king of a vast empire. The empire was in disarray and its fundamental deficiency was its previous king's inability to unite the people. Potential said the people were from all over the world and came to this kingdom because it held hope for a better future. He said the new king possessed a scroll that held "The Vision," but only the one who was worthy could read it. Faith tells of how she heard the story and thought it was something that he heard at school, but soon found out that Potential had dreamed this story. She soon realized that this dream was a foreshadowing of things to come.

When Potential turned thirteen he began to work with his father, Action, in the family business. The family business, Possibility Mart, supplied food for the people of Trustworthy County for centuries and was the only supermarket that town had ever known. Action knew that Potential possessed many skills, from running a business to being able to lead others with ease, but those skills alone were not going to make Potential the man his father felt he was destined to become. Faith always believed that Potential would become a great man, but

Action constantly pushed Potential to put forth his full effort in all that he did because Action understood that knowledge is not power. It's the application of that knowledge that is power. Potential could know all the skills he possessed his whole life, but until he actually displayed those skills in everyday life, they meant nothing. So Potential began diligently working for his father and soon had the opportunity to meet a young man who would change the course of his life. Future business partner and soon to be best friend, HW, also known as Hard Work Johnson, became an employee at Possibility Mart. They would talk about everything while they were on the job – school, parents, love. Nothing was off limits.

One afternoon, they began talking about the supermarket business and HW told Potential that there was better quality food that Action could sell to the people of Trustworthy County. He said that he had gone to Equalityville and they had similar food, but it was of a higher quality. HW said the food that the people of Trustworthy County had been eating for so long is good, but there are so many varieties of the same food that they had never heard of before. He went on to say that there are more colors of apples than just red, there are more flavors of potato chips than just regular, and there are different ways you can make chicken. It can be fried, baked, sautéed, and so on. He said that all these choices (most of which Potential did not even know existed) made the experience of eating so much more enjoyable and full for the people of Equalityville. They woke up excited about breakfast. They looked forward to having dinner in the evening. At this point HW got really excited and said that more than anything they understood the food. They appreciated the food for what it had to offer. Just by having variety and being open to that variety, they learned how to make meals that helped people improve concentration and live longer. Now anyone who knows Potential knows two things are very important to him: family and being right. Potential usually laughs at this part of the story because he said he felt he had two choices, to knock HW out for disrespecting his family business or look more into what he was talking about. It was at this point that Potential realized he had to travel to Equalityville to see for himself.

When Potential told his mother and father about the journey he would soon embark upon, his parents were not happy, to say the least. Now eighteen, Potential was supposed to go straight to college and gain the skills necessary to run Possibility Mart just as it had been run for the past four generations. Action explained how Trustworthy County relied on their family for everything that they ate and if he did not learn the skills necessary to continue the business exactly how it was always run, the county people may starve. Potential realized that this was surely a scare tactic, because there were others in the county that Action had taught to replicate the business and they would be able to provide the same services. Potential explained that it wasn't that he wanted out of the business but, on the contrary, he wanted to offer the people of Trustworthy County something better, something different.

As upset as Action was at Potential's fervent desire to change the family business, he could not help but see himself in Potential. He tried to change the business when he was around Potential's age, but Potential's grandfather, Tradition Smith, would not approve. Action eventually gave in to his father's wishes and kept the business exactly the same. Action and Faith discussed it and decided to compromise. Potential would have one year to learn everything he needed to learn in Equalityville. Afterwards, he had to return to the county, go to college, and start running the family business.

So with Action, Faith, and Hard Work backing him, Potential began his journey to Equalityville. When Potential finally reached Equalityville, he was amazed at what he saw. It was a totally different world. The streets looked different. The buildings looked different. The people looked different. It was as if everything he knew and saw in Trustworthy County had been given a facelift. Everything looked upgraded. He wondered what gave people this glow most of them exuded.

When Potential arrived at Diversity Supermarket, he immediately saw that HW was right! There were so many different ways to make the same food that his family had been making for centuries. It was amazing. He immediately asked for the store manager. He explained his desire to learn their

27

business and improve his family business in Trustworthy County. At first, the manager seemed apprehensive because he had heard that the people of Trustworthy County were sometimes difficult students. It was hard for them to accept different ways of doing things. But he liked Potential's eagerness to learn, so he hired him as an apprentice.

Potential knew that he only had one year to learn everything he needed to know so he worked diligently for twelve hours a day, six days a week. He learned everything, from the types of foods that the deli had to the manner in which the manager hired employees. Potential was more focused than any apprentice or employee ever hired. However, little did the manager or Potential know, but Potential's focus was about to broaden slightly.

About six months into working at Diversity Supermarket, in walked Christina Reality. As soon as she entered the management office where Potential often read during his breaks, he knew that he might be witnessing beauty in its most pure form. Potential always told this story with such energy that the listener thought she descended from heaven rather than walked through the door of a supermarket. Potential always said that he knew he had to say something to her because this might be his one opportunity to talk with someone this beautiful. So he mustered up his courage and said the smoothest line he could think of: "Hi." Though Christina was very beautiful, she never wanted to come across as arrogant. She always took the time to speak with others and be cordial. Plus, Potential wasn't that bad looking himself and caught her attention. As they talked, he realized that she was the daughter of the owner of Diversity Supermarket. She was being groomed to assume ownership of the business one day. When she heard his story, they could not believe how much they had in common. As the next six months passed, they spent plenty of time with one another. By the end of Potential's one-year apprenticeship, he had not only acquired a wealth of knowledge, but he had also acquired a fiancé.

When Potential returned home, his parents anxiously awaited to meet Christina Reality. The first thing that Action and Faith noticed in her was that characteristic glow of the people of Equalityville. At first this worried them, but after spending time with Christina, Potential's parents welcomed her into the family with open arms. They planned to marry within the year, but there was one problem. Christina was Mr. Reality's only child and he said that his family name would not die, so the man she married would have to hyphenate his last name to include Reality. When Potential first heard this he thought of two options: he could tell Mr. Reality a thing or two about what he thought about hyphenating his name or he could realize that Christina's presence in his life was too important to gamble with and accept the request. Potential once again made the wiser decision and accepted her father's request.

On February 14, 1944, Christina and Potential wed and became Mr. and Mrs. Potential Becomes Reality-Smith. Christina decided to live in Trustworthy County with Potential because she knew she could help make Potential's family business stronger and bigger than anyone ever imagined. Over the next four decades, Potential and Christina created the largest supermarket business in history. They not only fed people from Trustworthy County, but people from all over the world traveled to their supermarket to experience food in a way they had never experienced it before. The demand spread so far that they had to develop chains of supermarkets in countries all over the world. To this day their supermarket remains the highest grossing store in history because of their simple philosophy: to appreciate food in all of its different shapes, colors, and mixtures and to apply this knowledge to the food they provided. They brought their philosophy of appreciation of differences to the political arena, home life, and other men and women. As a result, more and more people began to display this glow – the glow of enlightenment. People were happier and more fulfilled. It was simply amazing what one man's life created. A concept so simple, but constantly overlooked. It took the wisdom of one ordinary man to unlock this knowledge and teach the world how to live extraordinary lives.

As I look out over this crowd today, I can't help but stand in awe of the influence one man's life has had on so many. Because of Potential there is hope in the ghetto for a better life. Because of Potential there is faith that a broken family can be made whole. There is a sincere belief in a better tomorrow because Potential existed and continues to exist. As I look into each of your faces, I can't help but see Potential. I can't help but notice that smile of gratefulness Potential possessed for today and the eyes of hopefulness Potential had for tomorrow.

Potential was born into this world just like all of us. With the guidance of Action and Faith and the steady friendship of Hard Work, Potential began to understand the gift he was given. Potential's understanding was actualized when he met Christina and he became Potential Becomes Reality-Smith. Potential's gift is the same gift each of us has. No matter our age, race, religion, gender, or place of origin, Potential lives in us. It's up to each of us whether our Potential will meet Reality.

Chapter 2:
Choice

"For what is the best choice, for each individual is the highest it is possible for him to achieve."

~ Aristotle

A friend once told me a story of two brothers who lost their father to alcoholism. One son, Jake, grew up to follow the same turbulent path as his father and fell prey to the seduction of the bottle. The other son, Ryan, grew up in the same home as his brother, but instead attended an elite university and became a successful businessman. When Jake was asked why he turned out the way he did, he replied, "My father was an alcoholic. What else was I supposed to become?" Ryan was asked the same question and replied, "My father was an alcoholic. What else was I supposed to become?" The ability to choose is uniquely human. In many ways, it separates us from every other living creature that walks the earth. If we want to live somewhere that is uninhabitable in its current state, then we choose to build homes and create a more livable environment. If we want to defy nature and do something that we are physically incapable of doing, then we choose to create machines like airplanes and cars that can take us higher and faster then we could ever go on two feet. As humans, we can choose to overcome limitations.

What gives us this ability to overcome? When all the strengths that we hold as humans are stacked side by side, without a doubt our distinguishing feature is the mind. Our minds give us the ability to learn new ways to tackle challenges by reworking bad situations and creating something that makes our lives a little easier. Unlike animals', our minds give us the chance to adapt and potentially have a degree of control in any situation. Philosopher Napoleon Hill insightfully observed, "Anything the mind can conceive and believe ... it can achieve."

"Anything" is a powerful word. The history of the human race shows the sheer magnificence and beauty that can spring from the mind believing *anything*. The Egyptians believed they could build homes for the afterlife that would withstand the test of time, and as a result we still enjoy the beauty of the pyramids thousands of years later. A small band of revolutionaries believed in a government that bestowed equal rights upon all men even if it meant war with one of the most powerful countries in the world, and America was born. A nonviolent movement for justice, an information system that connects the world, and flights to celestial bodies are each a testament to humans believing amazing things and achieving that much more.

However, the dangerous side of *anything* is that the mind also has the ability to believe and achieve the darkest and most terrifying acts. One man believed that he could assume control of a country, and eventually the world, by eradicating one race of people, and the Holocaust was etched in history. A group of men believed that people from the "dark continent" were no more than animals and the slave trade became one of the most inhumane practices in history. A woman is raped; a soon-to-retire grandfather is the victim of a white-collar crime and loses his pension; a child is neglected and left for dead. Each is evidence that the pendulum of possibility can swing either way when the human mind is involved.

The constant in both the magnificence and horror of *anything* is one simple word: choice. Some choose to give the world their special gifts to make it better; others decide to use their talents to contribute to the downward spiral of others. Many fall somewhere between these ends of the spectrum. The question that always follows a significant decision is, *Why did the person make that choice?* This question is particularly interesting in challenging situations that require tough decisions.

As young adults, we are bombarded with such situations as we transition into adulthood. We ask ourselves questions like *Will I accept a guaranteed job offer after school or take a risk and follow my dream?* and *Is this person worth a long-distance relationship or am I better taking my chances as a single where I live?* and *Are my parents right about saving money and living at home or should I just travel the world with my friends like I originally planned?* Each dilemma presents a unique challenge, but provides the chance to choose a path that can significantly impact our lives. Each dilemma incites excitement at the prospect of making a bold decision, while summoning a cautionary anxiety about the potential dangers of a poor decision. Despite the inner turmoil that frequently accompanies tough decisions in life, how we reach a final choice often remains a mystery. Thus, the question arises, *What drives our choices?*

Curious Circumstances

When Ryan, the second brother from my friend's story, left home to begin his first year in graduate school, he was likely astonished by his accomplishment. Despite suffering through his father's drunken rants about how life is unfair, hearing his mother sob as her family spiraled out of control, and experiencing an emotional breakdown that nearly drove him to take his life, Ryan overcame an extremely difficult life situation and stood at the threshold of achieving the unimaginable: becoming a businessman.

Jake, Ryan's brother, saw a completely different future ahead. After being arrested for the fifth time for driving under the influence, Jake's license was revoked. Unable to drive, Jake found it difficult to find work. His transportation problems, lack of a high school diploma, and history of unreliability and unprofessionalism made him a less-than-desirable employee for any business in his small suburban town. Jake saw one solution: drinking. Despite their shared turbulent upbringing, Ryan and Jake chose diverging paths.

While the details of our lives may not match the intensity of Ryan's and Jake's, challenges force each of us to make difficult decisions. Whether they are rooted in family life, academic abilities, or emotional stability, our challenges shape our perspectives and choices. The surroundings that birth our individual challenges often include others' expectations for handling these difficult situations, personal expectations, and resources that can help us. While expectations can play a tremendous role, the resources that are available to help us overcome challenges may provide the most insight into how our decisions eventually materialize. Resources like family counseling, academic tutoring, or emotional support may be the deciding factors for whether we overcome challenges or buckle under their weight. The numbers of resources available to our generation and their applications have drastically changed compared to previous generations.

As young adults of the twenty-first century, one of our biggest decisions was where to attend college. I remember the grueling routine of researching schools and slowly narrowing down the list to a manageable ten to fifteen schools; the list provided variety while ensuring I would be accepted somewhere. The decision to go to college reflected my parents' expectations that I "do something with my life," my friends' expectations that I follow a path like theirs, and my personal expectations to continue school and learn more about the field I wanted to pursue – psychology.

While these expectations contributed to my final decision on a school, I also considered more practical issues. I wondered how I would pay for schools that did not offer financial aid. I explored whether the schools had my major. I contemplated where I would live if accepted. I obsessed about my personal academic abilities and whether they would guarantee acceptance. Each issue spoke to the resources I had available to make my decision. If I did not have enough money, then I likely would have searched for a job instead of a school. If a school did not have my major or housing for freshmen, then I probably would not have considered that school. If I didn't test well and achieve decent grades then all my efforts to attend a top-notch school would be futile. These factors played a significant role in my decision-making process.

According to observers of historical shifts and societal trends, our generation has more access to resources for making informed decisions than any previous generation due to the technology at our disposal. Some insist that technologies ranging from microwave ovens to smartphones give our generation more options in every arena of life. A quick search on the Internet for colleges during my junior year of high school was proof of this. Not only did it give me hundreds of choices for schools, but a few more minutes of searching yielded just as many ideas and programs for paying tuition. Whether it's student loans or scholarships, our generation has vast financial resources available for college. Despite some economic bumps during our lifetime, most of us who are able to attend college come from families that can provide us with a degree of financial stability. Since resources are a driving force for making choices and we have them available to us, then the question for many of us is, *Are we using the available resources?*

People fall into one of two categories: *users* or *non-users*. As the names indicate, users try to use the resources available, while non-users do not. Resources include money, the people in our social and professional networks, and the ability to spot opportunities. Even when minimal resources are available, each person can use or neglect them. Exploring what makes users and non-users tick may shed light on what drives their choices.

Unusually Resourceful

By anyone's estimation, Ryan was a talented guy. By the time he started high school, he was already reading at a twelfth-grade level and had successfully begun a neighborhood lawn mowing business with the slogan, "If we don't cut it, we'll cut you ... a deal." Despite little support at home for his plans to attend college, Ryan sought a college counselor during his sophomore year, enrolled in five advance placement courses his junior year, and used his business earnings to pay college application fees. He used every resource at his disposal to graduate high school and attend college.

Jake, on the other hand, had a knack for avoiding work. Naturally intelligent and charismatic like his brother, Jake used his talents to steal cigarettes and beer from the local grocery store for his high school buddies. When confronted by his mother about misbehavior and poor schoolwork, he would snidely respond that his grades were "no worse than Dad's drinking problem." Over time, Jake began to emulate the erratic antics that characterized his father's lifestyle. By senior year of high school, the mounting home and school problems defeated any desire Jake had to overcome these challenges and instead became the spark for a lifelong partnership with alcohol. The separate paths Ryan and Jake took provide a glimpse into the inner workings of users and non-users.

In many ways, Jake's approach resembled the style of the Whatevers. When confronted by his mother, agitated by his father's drinking, or pressured to act more like his brother, Jake's responses were generally "Whatever." Whether Jake was aware of it or not, his actions suggested that not dealing with his problems was the solution he preferred. He may have thought it freed him from making tough decisions. Psychologist William James noted that "when you have to make a choice and don't make it, that is in itself a choice." The implication of "choosing not to choose" is a hotly debated topic, particularly in reference to our generation. Some cultural commentators argue that the nonchalance within our generation breeds apathy. They believe our generation may neglect the most important issues related to human progress simply because "we don't care."

The arguments against this perspective often delve into *how* users use resources. While Ryan used his intelligence and ability to earn money to achieve his goal, his style for handling challenges likely influenced whether he continued to pursue his dream. These arguments urge us to observe those of us who are Nonstoppers or Knows. Whether we're developing an online business or working an extra fifteen hours a week petitioning for a social cause, our generation also represents a new breed of go-getters. However, the praise this elicits is tempered by warnings about the anxiety and sense of entitlement that Nonstoppers and Knows may reveal. Nonstoppers' push to overcome challenges and face tough decisions may lead to such overwhelming anxiety that making choices becomes a burden instead of an opportunity. On the other hand, the confidence of the Knows may lead them to overestimate their decision-making ability. In other words, users come closer to making tough decisions than non-users, but run the risk of forfeiting progress due to debilitating anxiety or a sense of entitlement.

The non-users' and users' approaches to tough decisions show the considerations each group takes into account when presented with options. One person may choose not to choose. Another may use several options to make a difficult decision and triumph. Still, does something more truly represent the driving force behind our choices?

Undying Pursuit

From birth, Ryan and Jake faced many challenges. Early in both their lives, they adopted different ways to handle the stress of their family. Jake often cried about the lack of attention, while Ryan entertained himself. What is most fascinating about Ryan's and Jake's stories is that the same circumstances surrounded each. Both had the same resources available, even if they were minimal. Yet each chose different life directions.

If the circumstances and available resources do not fully account for how we arrive at a choice, then what does? Victor Frankl was a world-renowned doctor, therapist, and philosopher, and a holocaust survivor. During his time in a concentration camp, he tried to help others from breaking down mentally and committing suicide. What he observed was that people found a reason to keep living. Despite the horrors and severely limited resources, people found the energy to keep moving forward and find meaning in their suffering. In *Man's Search for Meaning*, Frankl concluded, "Everything can be taken away from a man but one thing: the last of the human freedom – to choose one's attitude in any given set of circumstances, to choose one's own way."

The conclusion is that attitude is the driving force. Attitude is the lens a person sees a situation through and the guiding force for handling challenges. When we think of a more efficient way to complete a project, decide to spend more time with family, or choose to relax for one day during the week, isn't it our attitude that sparks these actions? The attitudes of the Whatevers, Nonstoppers, and Knows are the basis for whether they notice the resources available or develop the resolve to face and overcome challenges.

What is it about certain attitudes that push us past difficult life situations? What does a person need in order to use resources that others overlook? We need passion. Passions are attitudes that are turned up a notch. They reflect a deep belief that we are working toward something important and we will push forward in good times and bad times. Passions are what allow us to squeeze everything that is good out of any situation. Isn't passion what we're searching for? When we go to school, travel the world, or begin a job, aren't we looking for that "something" that will give us the feeling that life is worth living?

Do we suffer through life? Do we float by in mediocrity with few highs or lows? Do we enjoy every moment? Regardless, isn't it up to each of us how we act and react? Passion guided one of the greatest leaders of the twentieth century out of the bleakest of situations. Nelson Mandela served twenty-seven years in prison for opposing the inhumane practice of apartheid in his homeland of South Africa. Despite the prejudicial treatment he endured, Mandela refused to live his life in bitterness, but instead chose to forgive those who persecuted him. This attitude fueled his presidential campaign and eventually facilitated reconciliation between a divided South Africa.

While our generation has unprecedented resources and higher expectations for our lives than any previous generation, are we making the best choices? We believe in following our passions, but do we go about it in the best way? Do we look to our circumstances to guide us too often? Do we need to prepare our attitudes for our circumstances instead of the other way around? Are we, as individuals and as a generation, choosing the right attitudes?

Interlude:
Integrity

I used to put on different faces,
When I went to different places.
"Who are you now?"
Others would wonder aloud.
I replied, "I'm just being me...
Or at least what the situation calls me to be."
It was hard to tell where I stood,
Because every word I spoke was because I should.
It was not necessarily what I thought or believed,
Instead, it was whatever opened the door to opportunity.

Whether it was the opportunity to move up the corporate ladder
Or just get what I wanted from someone because I made them feel better,
My words rarely dug deeper than the superficial banter
Because my actions usually did not back up the chatter.
Some would get mad at this,
While others would just call me a hypocrite.
I brushed it off because they did not know the real me,
But to be honest, the *real* was even hard for me to see.
I had played role after role for so long
That I forgot who I was or where I belong.

I searched east and west, north and south, high and low
For someone to help me figure out which way to go.
I looked to my job, cash, and education
For answers and some kind of explanation.
I did not get what I needed so I asked friends and family,
They had some good answers, but it did not reveal me amply.
I looked within for some assurance and a glimpse of the real me,
But all I could find were empty words that kept the answers hiding.

Finally, I looked beyond myself for some help.
Some call it a transcendent experience I felt,

But at the end of the day I was almost certain
That what I found led my words and actions to complete
convergence.

I use to put on different faces,
When I went to different places.
Then I found my footing on a stable foundation,
And the words I spoke represented less perpetration.
In many ways, I found out who I am,
By realizing that I'm just one piece of a bigger plan.
It feels so good to find the real me
And have my words and actions in synchrony.
From what I hear, many simply call what I have integrity.

Chapter 3:
Faith

"Faith is the pierless bridge supporting what we see unto the scene that we do not."

~ Emily Dickinson

Anything is possible. You just need a little faith. Has someone said this to you before? Maybe in a moment of self-doubt or during a bad situation from which escape was unlikely, someone told you to have a little faith that everything would work out for the best. Today, the word "faith" carries many different meanings. It can speak to hope in something that is unseen. It can mean trusting in an idea that science has yet to prove. It can represent a person's religious belief system. This last meaning often prompts the strongest reactions. Some hear the word "faith" and are immediately turned off. They associate it with the unscientific, divisive, or simply irrelevant. Others hear the same word and think of hope, connection with others, or a God who is concerned about the life of each individual. The feelings that can accompany each of these perceptions of faith range from intense disgust to overwhelming anxiety to indescribable joy. These reactions to faith suggest that it touches on one of the most sensitive aspects of the human experience: the values an individual holds.

Historically, faith has played an integral role in how people define themselves and view the world. Many of our parents and grandparents used their embrace of or opposition

to faith as the basis for teaching their children what is important. Those who embraced faith may have taught that faith
urges us to help others and appreciate the lives we are given,
while those opposing faith may have taught that unity with
others and an embrace of the present moment supersede the
existential strivings of a faith-focused life. Whether it is an intense debate between individuals representing liberal and
conservative political leanings or a heated discussion with parents about who is appropriate to date, often underlying the
dialogue is a struggle to assert individual values. While many
factors influence how our values develop, few have the potential to impact our complete value system and worldview as
strongly as faith.

When closely examining many of the pivotal shifts in
history regarding civil rights, political change, and economic
development, the individuals who led these movements often
were inspired by values birthed by various faith traditions. Yet
a re-examination of these shifts in history also reveals that
when people received information that clearly indicated a better approach to dealing with such tough issues, they were
willing to fight for change. Some believe that faith has become
less relevant over the last century as science and technology
provide avenues for answering some of life's toughest questions. As the first generation to experience fully the benefits of
unlimited access to information, this shift in sentiments regarding faith raises many questions: Can technology and
information access serve the same purposes as faith? Have we

progressed beyond faith? Yet faith is rarely discussed in our social circles, on our jobs, or in our schools, which begs one simple question: *Is faith really that important for our generation?*

Faith versus Religion

Before discussing whether faith is important to us, we need to ask a much more basic question: How do we define faith as a generation? Many believe that faith simply refers to a person's religion. Is it that simple? Are faith and religion the same? If they are, that may explain people's strong responses to the issue of faith. In the name of religion, the Crusades were fought throughout Europe and the Middle East for centuries, slavery was justified in the United States, and many forms of prejudice were supported and persist today. It seems that the laws of various religions provide the basis to oppress the weak, disenfranchised, and powerless. It becomes even more disheartening when we think of how religion seems to divide people who are on equal footing both socially and economically; it can cause people to disrespect others based solely on beliefs. With our increasing awareness of others' beliefs and practices in today's society, this narrow way of thinking does not sit well with many people.

What if, however, religion and faith are two different ideas? Both share the same moral laws and tenets, or life principles, to guide individuals' lives. These range from not lying and stealing to honoring one's parents and treating others with respect. What if, however, the distinction between religion and faith arises from how people *use* these life principles? What if religion allows people to use life principles in a misguided way? Maybe religion has become an exercise in finding loopholes in the life principles and preventing personal growth. Maybe religion no longer means understanding the purpose of these principles and living to fulfill this purpose. When someone uses the life principles as the basis for hating others or disparaging those who are suffering, then the life principles are being mishandled, and maybe those practicing religion are mishandling them.

What about faith? I think of faith as an experience much deeper and personal than religion. I think of the same set of life principles that undergird religion, but used very differently. Faith focuses on understanding the meaning behind the life principles *and* assumes a willingness to use these principles to improve one's self and help others. Instead of using the life principles to rationalize criticism, those who have faith use the life principles to grow personally and to cherish all people because their experience is bigger than any one individual. The experience of faith can be a connection to a higher power, to a group of people, or to the universe. Regardless, the life principles are used to inspire self-improvement and enhance others' lives.

Thus, the difference between religion and faith seems to be the *use* of life principles. They can come from Christianity, Islam, Judaism, Hinduism, Buddhism, or another belief system, but their *application* has the impact on our personal lives and the lives of others. Thus, there can be Christians who practice religion and Christians who practice faith, Muslims who practice religion and Muslims who practice faith, and Jewish people who practice religion and Jewish people who practice faith. Those who use life principles to mistreat people while exalting themselves seem to me to practice religion. However, those who use these life principles to better themselves and those around them seem to me to practice faith.

A Moment of Reflection

A distinction between religion and faith is valuable, but still does not shed light on how and why faith is specifically important for our generation. What makes faith relevant for us? I've asked this question many times, but it comes up the most when I feel a bit lost. And there is no situation in which I feel more lost than on a first date. Getting ready, thinking about what to say, and figuring out where to go is a nerve-racking process. I remember one first date in particular; I could not do anything right. I was going out with a woman my friend told me was way out of my league, which made me even more anxious. In trying to impress her, we went to a place that was way over budget for someone whose gourmet meals usually consisted of ramen noodles and easy mac. After a night full of awkward silences from corny jokes ("That waitress doesn't have anything on you," referring to a 300-pound man), it was time to pay the bill. I went into my wallet for at least thirty seconds looking for money I did not have. After about forty-five seconds of fumbling through my wallet and avoiding eye

49

contact, my date finally asked whether I wanted to split the bill. I thought to myself, *Isn't this the twenty-first century? Don't you want to pay the whole bill?* Then I realized I wasn't thinking to myself but talking out loud. There was no second date (but I did get a free meal).

What does this story have to do with faith? Other than praying that this catastrophe would not get back to my friends (it did), the date forced me to think about what I did wrong and what I could do better on future dates. Did I follow the dating rules for first dates? Did I even know what the dating rules were for first dates? What did my date expect me to do? Why did I not get a second date? These questions required some self-examination and admitting to some tough truths. I definitely violated a couple of first-date rules. I should have been prepared to pay for the meal if I asked her out and picked the restaurant. I probably could have cut back on the bad jokes after a few awkward silences and instead asked her questions to get to know her better. Finally, it definitely was not cool to ask my date if she had any friends I could meet after I realized she and I were not going to work out.

One characteristic of faith is its emphasis on self-improvement. To improve anything, we need to know what's not working. The life principles are usually pretty good at helping us think about what's not working. Do not murder, do not commit adultery, and do not lie force us to think about where we stand. For instance, is an occasional lie acceptable when it spares someone from hurt? Regardless of our answer,

the life principles help us reflect on how we measure up personally and whether our actions lead to the outcomes we want.
They nudge us toward self-reflection in a world that sometimes
moves at such a pace that self-reflection is more of a luxury
than a necessity.

Self-reflection can lead many places. We may realize
that we acted against a life principle. Though our act fulfilled a
desire at the time, it weighed on our conscience and became
too much work to hide. We had to think of another lie to cover
up the first one. We looked at ourselves in the mirror with
some dissatisfaction because we hurt someone in ways difficult
to repair. Alternatively, self-reflection may lead us to see how
following life principles is tough initially, but seems to pay off
in the end. Maybe we told someone a tough truth that hurt at
the time, but we slept a little bit better that night because it
was the honest thing to do. Regardless of what we self-reflect
upon, faith gives us a way to think about who we truly are as
individuals.

Some people feel that the sole purpose of life principles
is to make us feel bad about who we are. While they can help
us reflect on what is not working, the other part of the equa-
tion is that they can show us who we can become. They can
call on us to become better people in every area of our lives.
We can become people who treat others with respect, people
who are honest with others and ourselves, and people who put
others first. Instead of highlighting the negatives, the life principles can become the guiding light for making us better

people. In this light, faith becomes an instrument of hope because of its appeal to our better natures. If life principles guided by faith are used in this manner, does faith become a little more relevant for a generation that seeks constant self-improvement and a better future?

A Lovely View

Love is a powerful word. We hear it all the time – when people talk about food, cars, television shows, and just about anything else they can enjoy for more than five seconds. Most of the time people use it lightly, to emphasize how much they like a particular place or object. Yet this word becomes almost reverential when applied to people. When we love another person we will do *anything* for that person. This is why most are reluctant to tell another person "I love you." It often takes a lifelong friendship, a familial bond, or a shared tragic experience for most people to tell others they are loved. For romantic relationships, it usually takes more than a couple of dates and boxes of chocolates for most people to acknowledge they have fallen in love. Yet when it happens, it truly is like *falling* in love. It is as if self-control is no longer an option. The free fall is so exciting and beautiful that the only worthwhile thought, action, or breath involves some aspect of the loved one.

If the word "love" can fuel an unquenchable romantic passion for another person, can we establish a relationship between it and faith? Faith focuses on empowering individuals to better the lives of others. There is a shared life principle that urges us to treat others as we want to be treated – the Golden Rule. The Golden Rule calls on us to see the true value of others as humans and treat them as such. While romantic love involves a free fall into love that is almost uncontrollable, the Golden Rule stands for a conscious decision to treat others with dignity, respect, compassion, and, in essence, love. This decision often manifests in three ways: acceptance, conviction, and service.

(Disclaimer: The following is not an attempt to give the meaning of love, but instead to describe what the "Golden Rule of love" looks like through the lens of faith. The meaning of love is beyond the scope of this book – and way over my head.)

For many, the word "judgment," and not "acceptance," is the first word they associate with people who profess using life principles to help others, but actually are using them to rationalize hurtful criticism. Many of us hold memories of feeling inadequate or belittled when meeting people who claim adherence to these principles, but whose actions are completely inconsistent. Are these memories instances of life principles being used in a misguided way? Instead of using life principles as a checklist of requirements, doesn't the Golden Rule call people guided by faith to learn more about others by first acknowledging their shared human experience?

When we accept others, we help them feel welcome and at ease. We give them the freedom to reveal their true identities because they feel valued. We care enough to listen to rants about the frustrating job, disappointing relationships, and the joys and tragedies of life. We care enough to offer help that can truly lead to a better life. Without acceptance, this connection never happens.

With this connection, people are willing to receive help. Thus, the logical next step is to share whatever can help and the second manifestation of the Golden Rule of love appears: conviction. Conviction is not a word we hear too often outside the courtroom, yet it is associated with more than fallen politicians or a pop icon's misbehavior. In the context of faith, conviction represents an unshakeable belief strengthened and supported by experience. If self-improvement can be traced back to faith and the life principles guided by faith, does it make sense to share these same helpful tools with others who want help? If faith urges someone to deal honestly with others, isn't the logical way to help someone to suggest that he stop lying? While this may seem logical, it can be viewed as judgmental. It is a thin line to walk. However, faith suggests that conviction is based on who a person can *become*, whereas judgment is convicting who a person *is*. Even though it is difficult to advise a person to stop lying, if lying is the root of the problem, then isn't suggesting the person live honestly the only way to help? In the end, to better the lives of others, faith-based action must be supported by acceptance and conviction.

The final component of the Golden Rule of love is service. Service plays a major role in our generation's lives. We are required to complete community service for school, we note service to the community on our résumés, and some of us

54

join organizations like the Peace Corps or Teaching Fellows™. While these kinds of service help others immeasurably, the service inspired by the Golden Rule of love involves every aspect of our lives and is not limited to a short-term commitment or occupation. It is an ever-present willingness to help someone else. Without getting involved with bettering others' lives, how will those who *want* help begin to improve themselves?

History repeatedly gives examples of how acceptance, conviction, and service spurred by faith are powerful tools for knocking down the walls of prejudice, bias, and hatred. Dr. Martin Luther King, Jr., was not alone in the American civil rights movement. Many valiant civil rights heroes fought for equality, but none had as broad an impact as Dr. King. Mahatma Gandhi faced one of the most immovable systems in history – the caste system, which was embedded in a society colonized by the British. The caste system forced people to live according to the family they were born into, even if that meant living like animals. It also forced all members of society to endure the oppression that comes with colonization. The outrage of people inside and outside India highlighted that this represented a clear violation of human rights. Yet it was Gandhi who was able to inspire a nation to change its ways and move toward a more peaceful coexistence.

What is it about these individuals that enabled them to spur such great change? Was it their speaking skills? Was it their ambition to become great? Was it their ability to acquire power and tell others what to do? What was it? If we listen carefully to their words and understand their visions, we see a common theme. Dr. King and Gandhi wanted people to be seen as people. They wanted others to understand that hurting the people who Dr. King or Gandhi represented was to hurt people just like themselves and their loved ones. Their faith inspired them to help others understand how each person has a unique form of expression, appearance, or background but, at the end of the day, has the common thread of being human. We have the common thread of caring about what others think of us, of hurting when someone we care about hurts, and of wanting respect for who we are as human beings. Both Dr. King and Gandhi showed how love – seeing the true value of others – touched people and made them want to change for the better.

One of the most amazing transformations of our generation is our ability to accept people for who they are. We have sat through history classes and heard about the riots of the 1960s, which were triggered by people not accepting others based on the color of their skin. We have seen terrorism and violence caused by religious fundamentalists who refuse to tolerate the lives of those who do not agree with them morally. We have witnessed conversations in classes, at work, and sometimes at home that have involved someone saying or doing something hurtful to someone else just because the person is different. Many times these attacks on others come from a place that is the opposite of love: hate. Hate distorts how people view the world. People begin to see those they hate as less than human. They begin to believe these people do not deserve the respect given to most human beings. Hate blinds people to the true value of others.

While our generation has come a long way from this overt form of venomous hate, we cannot deny the continued presence of obstacles for seeing the true value of others. Whether it is our sly remarks about "those people" or not acknowledging the existence of others who are not important to us, many of our social circles, home lives, and schools still have barriers that continue to divide us. If faith has spurred change in the past, can our generation use faith to break down still more barriers to unity?

Hitting a Wall

In the romantic comedy *The Break-Up,* longtime couple Gary (Vince Vaughn) and Brooke (Jennifer Aniston) learn that love has its limits. Vaughn and Aniston portray a tormented couple who make everyone in their lives uncomfortable with arguments during game night and obvious attempts to make the other jealous. Still it is clear that neither is making progress. They feel unhappy, lost, insecure, and confused about their relationship. Each wants to recapture the moments in which they felt fulfilled and joyful about life. Yet it becomes increasingly clear that neither has a plan to make this happen. After exhausting every trick a romantic comedy can manage in two hours, they finally accept that they have reached their limit.

Limitations are difficult to acknowledge, yet surround us every day. Whether it is a limit on how fast we can commute to work, the number of tasks we can accomplish in an hour, or our knowledge of the future, limitations lurk in every crevice of our lives. What makes them so difficult are the unsettling feelings that often accompany them. When Vaughn and Aniston realized there was no hope for their relationship, they probably felt upset, frustrated, and sad. They probably felt a deep pain for what they had lost and insecure about their futures. These are feelings everyone experiences. Some of us wonder if we will still move toward our dream careers after rejection from graduate school. Others feel helpless when a loved one who is in trouble will not change regardless of interventions. Situations constantly arise that can leave us feeling lost and confused about the next step to take.

While faith speaks to potential in ourselves and others, the word "potential" implies that we'll run into obstacles. Thanks to technology, our generation has found more innovative ways to accomplish tasks and deal with challenges than any generation that preceded us. We wanted to connect with people any time, and cyber social networks came into existence. We needed our music, movies, and Internet to follow us everywhere, and the cell phone was transformed into a mobile home entertainment center. When we want to know how to travel somewhere, understand a math problem, or learn to cook a gourmet meal, we google it. With the development of new technologies that allow us to multitask more quickly and efficiently, many of us accomplish goals and overcome challenges unflinchingly.

Our generation has heard a single mantra our entire lives: *You can do and become anything that you want.* While the innovative and adaptive nature of our minds provides evidence for that statement, limitations and challenges beg the question, *How do we become and do **anything**?*

Fully Complete

Abraham Lincoln said, "I have been driven many times to my knees by the overwhelming conviction that I had nowhere to go. My own wisdom, and that of all about me, seemed insufficient for the day." Lincoln is one of the most revered presidents in United States history and is often credited for successfully guiding this country through its darkest hour. Still, he acknowledged that he did not have all the answers. He went even further to admit that many around him did not have all the answers. When questions arise from situations that highlight our limitations as human beings, many of us grasp for anything that can provide relief from the unsettling feelings that accompany unsettling questions. Some of us may have a drink or smoke to free our minds from the stress. Others may completely dive into school or work to distract from the hurt. Still others may rely on relationships to fill a seemingly everpresent emptiness. We try our best to find answers to move forward when challenging situations leave us feeling hurt and uncertain about the future. We search for somewhere secure to ground ourselves as we press toward our goals and try to overcome inevitable challenges.

The problem with most of our solutions is that each only partially or temporarily solves our problems. A drink may allow us to feel a sense of ease for the moment, but when we sober up the challenge is no less difficult. While a job or school may provide a welcome distraction during the day, when we lay in bed at night the problems bubble to the surface. Relationships make us feel complete in many ways, but there are times when another person cannot do or say anything to assure us that everything will turn out well. None of these solutions can dig deep enough to root out the uncertainty that fuels our unsettling feelings. Like kids playing tag in the schoolyard, we all need a base to run to for safety. We all need a secure base to ground us so the turbulence of life will not shatter our inner strength and leave us feeling more lost and confused than we can tolerate.

A secure base can absorb all the uncertainty of the future and make our deepest inner selves a sturdy foundation. *Can faith be that secure base?* If our physical and mental health is any indication that it can, science supports it. In the February 12, 2009, issue of *Time* magazine, Jeffrey Kluger's "The Biology of Belief" reported that scientists and doctors have found that faith-related activities have several positive effects on physical health. Prayer and meditation, practiced consistently over a long period, are related to permanent changes in the brain. While research is in the early stages, these changes appear to help people remain calmer and keep from becoming overwhelmed and stressed. Even more surprising for many of the scientists, faith was found to be related to longevity. Whether people eat healthier because they believe the body is sacred or belong to a faith community to help them feel connected to others, doctors' findings suggest that people who actively practice their faith live longer. The results of these studies were so compelling that many hospitals began to train doctors on how to discuss issues of spirituality when treating patients.

In terms of mental health, the hope that faith may provide in a distressing or traumatic situation has been linked to fewer symptoms of depression, anxiety, and stress. Specifically, psychologists have found that an individual's faith may help him interpret bad situations or unhappy events in a way that makes the situation meaningful. In other words, when people lose their jobs, get a bad grade, or divorce, faith can become a tool to deal with the hurt, to see the positive in the situation, and to grow from the challenges. Whether it is the support provided by others in the faith community during hard times or a simple feeling of confidence that everything will turn out OK, scientists keep finding support for the positive effects of faith on mental health.

The physical and mental health benefits of faith gain further strength when we consider the philosophical arguments for faith as a secure base. While science has answered many important questions, many scientists believe that it will never be able to answer the questions that perplex us most. In his compelling book *The Language of God*, Francis Collins details why faith is not in opposition to scientific findings like evolution and stem-cell research, noting that many important questions remain unanswered. As the former head of the Human Genome Project, Collins concedes that science's knowledge of the human body is far from an explanation of what happens when we die or why we have a moral conscience. He argues that these are questions only faith can answer.

A problem with faith answering these questions, however, lies in the word itself. The dictionary definition of faith is "to believe." Must answers simply be believed to be true? Our generation does not often believe for the sake of believing. We have the Internet to check every perspective on issues. We have professors and parents who tell us to think critically about life and not accept anything at face value. We naturally question authority and are confident about what we need to know and what we can disregard. We are skeptical about anything that requires us just to believe; in fact, many doubt. Yet many who subscribe to faith as an answer to tough questions believe doubt is not mutually exclusive with faith. In his seminal book *The Case for Faith*, journalist Lee Strobel suggests that doubt can signal that a person is actively trying to understand faith and its potential as a secure base. Others suggest that trusting in faith for the answers will not happen unless a person experiences faith as providing the answers.

This became vividly clear to me during my second year of graduate school. While approaching the end of my second semester, within the span of a couple of days, I learned of my grandfather's passing and the end of my aunt's battle with lung cancer. As a pallbearer in both funerals, I had the chance to say an intimate goodbye that spurred reflection on the finite nature of human life. At first, I became numb and tried not to think about it. I plunged into school work and exercise to keep my mind distracted. That worked for a little while, but my mind always drifted back to the losses. I had so many questions. My aunt never smoked, so why did she succumb to lung cancer? Where is my grandfather now? Why did I have to experience two losses in one week? The more questions I had, the deeper my despair and pain became. I searched for comfort from others, but there was not much anyone could say to console me. I retreated to the privacy of my journal and poured every agonizing and confused emotion onto those pages.

As time passed, I realized that the weight of the pain was too much to carry. It was affecting every area of my life. As a budding psychologist, I wanted to focus on providing the best care for my clients. My friends and family needed someone in their lives who was not constantly distracted by his own thoughts. I needed to become free of a burden that I did not have the power to unload. It was at this desperate point that I decided to try faith. I prayed that God would give me the strength to move forward. Despite my reservations, I acknowledged that my loved ones were no longer suffering and there was a purpose for their passing. With each step toward faith, I felt my load lighten. As I relied on the faith that I was initially reluctant to acknowledge, I experienced a deepening peace that a job, school, alcohol, friends, or family could not spark. It was a peace that words could not describe.

In the end, I learned what separates faith from every other option available for answering life's toughest questions and dealing with life's biggest challenges. Simply put, it is because faith is based upon a relationship with something greater than us. It is a relationship that inspires us to become better by causing us to reflect upon life principles and strive to achieve more. It is a relationship that provokes a person to see the true value in others and treat them accordingly. It is a relationship that allows for our limitations as human beings but still urges us to use every resource available to handle difficult situations. It is a relationship that develops trust over time by allowing us to experience security about the future despite the challenges.

Faith is also a relationship that requires the first step to come from the individual. Faith does not require us to do all the work, not even most of it, but it does require us to initiate the relationship. Dr. King once described faith as "taking the first step even when you don't see the whole staircase."

As young adults of the twenty-first century, we constantly face expectations and challenging situations that threaten how secure we feel about the future. Many of us want to graduate at the top of our class, so we are tempted to lose a few hours of sleep each night for the sake of extra study time. We want to remain connected with our friends, so we feel pressure to hang out at this party, visit that country, or bar hop even if we don't have the money or the time. Our parents, teachers, and neighbors expect us to find a job that will bring both prestige and a sufficient salary, not realizing that this pursuit can cause a significant amount of stress. Every day we are pulled in different directions that require levels of energy that can undermine our health and ask us to meet expectations that sometimes counter who we are as individuals.

The unique strength of faith lies in its ability to bring consistency and stability to situations and people. Faith can potentially permeate every area of a person's life. It has the potential to inform our values while shaping our attitudes and outlook. It often inspires dignity, respect, and integrity. If philosopher and psychologist Erich Fromm's description of integrity as "a willingness not to violate one's identity" is accurate, then faith can also inspire us to remain true to ourselves despite the many expectations and challenges that try to dictate otherwise. By penetrating our inner depths, faith can connect us with an unshakeable foundation that provides answers when the questions are most dire.

Yet, doubt can discourage us from even exploring faith as an option. We might focus on what we lose by embracing faith, such as a particular lifestyle or reputation. We might find faith so elusive that we write it off as irrelevant. In fact, we might portray faith as dangerous because we believe it has the potential to cloud rationality.

More than any other generation, we value weighing our options and using every resource available to become better people. If this truly represents our values, then only exploring what we may lose by embracing faith is not enough or even consistent. The question must first be, *What do we stand to gain?*

Interlude:
Wakati

I HATE YOU!
But I can't escape you.
Yet you escape me constantly.
You're always leaving me!
No matter how much I try to hold on to you.
I'm told to cherish you,
But I don't listen.
I feel like I'll have you forever.
You'll always be mine ... right?
No you won't!
Don't lie to me with the seductiveness of youthful beauty,
Or the false security of money.
I've seen you leave others.
Sometimes you leave them as soon you meet
And sometimes it takes longer
But you always leave ... ALWAYS!
I must tell you,
I wouldn't be this upset if I didn't care about you.
You're too precious to let go without a fight.
I wake up every day with you on my mind,
Thinking about how I can right the wrongs I've done to you in
the past.
I suppose I deserve to have you leave.

As upset as I am at your departure,
I must admit,
You are quite fair.
You've been pretty equal to everyone.
It's everyone else that treats you differently.
Some have treated you like a queen.
They savor your presence
And acknowledge your existence.
They treasure your forward-moving persistence.
And for them you reward greatly.
If they respect you, their hearts' desires will be fulfilled.
But for those who don't understand you,
Those who will not befriend you,

You are an unforgiving ...
You catch my drift.
You don't get mad, sad, or glad.
You just keep moving further from me,
EXPRESSIONLESS!
I honestly feel that you don't care what I do.
When I used to look in your eyes, I saw hope.
Now, I don't know what I see.
It could be despair, desperation, and denigration,
But then I look again and see wisdom, experience, and past
moments of joy.

I like to call you by your pet name in Swahili, Wakati,
Because I feel like I truly understand you.
I just hope by me pouring out my heart to you,
Others will understand the truth.
We cannot take you for granted.
Because at this moment our lives are at their dawn
And when you're gone, you're gone.
So it is at this moment I will stop,
Even as you keep whispering "tick tock, tick tock."

Wakati is the Swahili word for "time."

Chapter 4:
Goals: A Work in Progress

Hope for the best, but prepare for the worst.

~ English Proverb

Do you remember the story of the tortoise and the hare? Aesop, a Greek slave from the seventh century B.C., put together stories that were intended to teach a lesson. Today, children around the world learn about *Aesop's Fables*. His fable about the tortoise and the hare stuck with me for some reason. Whether it was because the fable was particularly poignant or the fact that slaves in ancient Greece had time to write stories about animals talking to each other, I knew at the young age of five that this story had something important behind it. The fable begins with this annoying, arrogant hare running around boasting about how fast he is. While proclaiming his glory, he glimpses this tortoise slowly walking around in the forest. The hare could not resist making fun of this creature moving at a snail's pace. The tortoise hears the hare and challenges the hare to a race. Everyone in the forest gathers to see this spectacle. As soon as the whistle blows, both are off. The hare blasts out of the gate and is so far ahead of the tortoise halfway through the race that he decides to take a quick nap. The tortoise, on the other hand, decides to keep his steady pace. The quick nap becomes a deep slumber, and only the noise of cheering wakes the hare – just as the tortoise is about to cross the finish line. Despite summoning every bit of energy, the hare cannot catch up and the animals hail the tortoise as the new king of the forest.

This fable has been used for centuries in movies, books, and teachers' lesson plans to illustrate the moral that hard work and persistence pay off. The hare was not diligent and lost the race. It seems simple enough, but is that all there is to this story? Aesop's fable illustrates the concept of loyalty to a task and the grit to survive hardship, but is it relevant to our generation's quest to find a passion in life or realize our dreams?

Starting Line

Any race worth watching has at least two competitors who remain fairly close until the end. By anyone's estimation, the race between the tortoise and the hare was not likely to be competitive. Still, the tortoise challenged the hare to a race. What gave the tortoise the idea that he could possibly win? He had probably seen the hare leave competitors in the dust – the big bad gorillas, the speedy deer, and maybe even a lion or two who thought an easy meal was guaranteed. The hare had yet to face a challenger who could defeat him. Yet something about that day and the hare's teasing caused the tortoise to say, "That's it. I'm not taking it anymore. Let's race!" With those words, the tortoise and the hare moved to the starting line.

The taunts of the hare basically provoked the tortoise to action. What provokes someone to *do* something? Our generation is the generation of high expectations. Many of us have high expectations for ourselves and others have high expectations of us. We are expected to go to college and excel in a job that furthers our career and provides financial stability, in a profession that fulfills us personally and uses each of our unique talents. We are expected to expand our social networks while having rich, deep relationships with others, which involves much time and care. We juggle many seemingly contradictory expectations with the hope of meeting them all. Each of us has private ideas and secret dreams about what we want to do with our lives, but sometimes the dreams feel too impossible to give serious consideration. Opportunities may emerge, but for one reason or another they may not provoke us to *do* something. How do we manage having big dreams when reality does not always accommodate them?

One interesting aspect of this fable is that the tortoise challenged the hare and not vice versa. The tortoise could have ignored the hare and continued to wherever he was going. The hare had probably taunted him many times before, and many others like him. In the past, the tortoise and everyone else likely suffered through it. The hare defeated whoever tried to outrun him. Still, the tortoise challenged the hare to a race. Racing the tortoise and winning was a dream bigger than the reality of the situation. Yet the tortoise dared to have this dream and do something about it.

As soon as the tortoise opened his mouth to challenge the hare and made the forest aware of his big dream, I'm sure he received an abundance of "advice." The other tortoises probably told him that he had the tortoises' reputation to uphold and he was about to ruin it by racing the hare. The birds probably told him that they had flown over the race-course and thought it was much too difficult for the tortoise to stand a chance. The fish (who could not race even if they tried) may have laughed that the tortoise even imagined that he could race the hare and win. As the tortoise looked around, I'm sure he found very few animals supporting his big dream to race the hare. Frustration probably surfaced as the tortoise realized how little faith others had in his ability to win the race.

Then there were his personal insecurities. *Can I really race against the hare and have a respectable finish?* he may have thought. He may have wondered how tough the track was or what would happen if he became too tired or acciden-tally went in the wrong direction. He may have thought about his comfortable bed and being home sleeping, like he originally planned. Instead, he was entering this impossible race with a superior opponent and no support from anyone in sight. He may have started questioning his choice to dream big. In fact, he may have wondered where all of these reservations sudden-ly came from, but before he could think about it much longer he was already on the starting line.

In the search for that "thing" that will provoke us to do something, we can get so tangled in distractions that our big dream is completely overshadowed. People may suggest a cer-tain path, a particular school, or a job opportunity. People may offer a "shot of reality" by telling us we don't have what it takes to reach our dreams. They may laugh that we even dream that big. The distractions may also come from within – personal insecurities that make us feel we are not capable of achieving the dream. Every time there is a spark to take action, distractions may cause us to second-guess whether we really want to do something or if it is even worth pursuing.

Distractions can be well-intentioned: to keep us safe. The warnings and advice to turn in another direction often come from people in our lives who do not want to see us fail. Parents' fears about our future can overshadow our concern for our personal well-being. Even a friend who laughs at our dreams may be concerned that failure or success will change the friendship and is protecting the friendship without being aware of it. In ourselves, we naturally want to stay safe and do what is in our power to protect ourselves. Insecurities exist because we have real concerns about whether following a dream is the best idea. No one wants to fail. Insecurities force us to think about how likely it is we will realize the dream versus how difficult the road ahead is. Our decisions are often based upon what will place us in the best position in the end.

Safeguards are great, but they become distractions when we let them turn into a fear so intense that we never start the race. If someone is so concerned with a perfect report card that he does not take a difficult class that interests him, is so afraid of making a mistake in a relationship that she chooses to be alone, or is unwilling to share his dreams because people may laugh, then the safeguards have become distractions. Safeguards are there to help make smart decisions, not to *be* the decisions. If safeguards cause us to rethink whether something is worth doing once our interest is raised, then they have likely become distractions.

The problem with distractions is they distort reality. They make reality seem scarier than it actually is. Distractions can lead us to believe that making a mistake while striving for the big dream is fatal to the dream and our self-esteem. Distractions suggest that achieving anything different from the original goal means failure. If someone does something amazing but it does not exactly match the original big dream, then distractions can paint it as a failure. Distractions use mistakes as reasons to believe the dream will never materialize, instead of using lessons learned from mistakes as the building blocks for a plan to overcome obstacles. Distractions represent fears; they take the focus off the inspiration to do something and place it on what someone cannot do well.

Reality is different than the distortions caused by distractions. Perfection is usually not an option, and mistakes and challenges are likely. Some of the most surprising accomplishments in history have started with a mistake. In 1937, baker Ruth Wakefield was making one of her favorite cookie recipes, Butter Drop Do cookies, which date back to colonial times. She found herself short an ingredient, chocolate. She had a semisweet bar of chocolate on hand and cut it into small chunks and placed them in the dough. She assumed the chocolate would melt into the dough. Instead, the chocolate chunks held their shape and the first chocolate chip cookies were created. Similarly, Thomas Edison went through thousands of tests before finding the right material to create the light bulb. Coca-Cola®, Post-it® Notes, Silly Putty®, and many other inventions were the result of mistakes or accidents that occurred when people were trying to do something else. None of these great inventions would exist if the inventors did not start the process by *doing* something.

Despite the distractions that likely surrounded the tortoise, he was provoked enough to get on the starting line and begin the race with the goal of winning. *Webster's Dictionary* defines a goal as "the end toward which effort is directed." This idea of effort, in the case of the tortoise, began with his first step to the starting line. Poet Johann Wolfgang von Goethe wrote that "what is not started today is never finished tomorrow." As a generation, many of us were taught to think through our significant decisions and weigh the advantages versus disadvantages. While this process is important, it can cause us to contemplate an idea for so long that the desire or confidence to move toward the goal is lost. The effort necessary to reach the goal is never made. Isn't the dream, or goal, only as good as the effort we put forth? The process begins with that first little bit of effort. Effort is signing up for tryouts for the team while acknowledging it's a long shot. Effort is saying "hi" to a cute guy or girl, despite being unsure about how he or she feels. While being inspired and having a goal is important, it does not mean much if that first step is not taken. The tortoise could have dreamed of winning against the hare, but if he never challenged him and stepped up to the starting line, then his dreams would not amount to much more than fantasy.

As soon as the tortoise stepped up to the starting line, the whistle blew. They were off – at least the hare was. The tortoise heard the whistle blow, but even with all his desire and effort he could only move about an eighth of the speed of the hare. The hare zoomed off so quickly that the animals probably whispered to one another, "This is going to be even more pathetic than we expected." The tortoise immediately had the disadvantage, which was probably a pivotal moment in the race for him. He was still at the beginning and could decide it wasn't worth it and quit without wasting too much time or energy. His distractions probably were on the sidelines telling him they knew this would happen and he needed to get out of the race to preserve some of his dignity. The hare was too far ahead for the tortoise to gain lost ground. The bottom line is that the tortoise had a decision to make very early in the race. Should he keep pressing forward toward his goal despite the bleak outlook, or should he quit before he did too much damage to his reputation?

How many times have we overcome distractions and taken the first step toward our goal only to find a seemingly impossible obstacle standing in the way? For the tortoise, it was that his body did not allow him to move faster. When we finally take those acting lessons, or work with a tutor to improve our grades, or open up to someone we've always wanted to have a closer relationship with, it seems the money for classes runs out, or the tutor is moving to another state, or the person of interest is not showing the same kind of openness about her life. Regardless of the scenario, obstacles burst onto the scene and force us to make a very difficult decision: to move forward or turn back. A closer look at how our generation deals with goals is necessary to understand how many of us make this decision.

Three groups of people, who many peg as hallmarks of our generation, were introduced in chapter 1: the *Knows,* the *Whatevers,* and the *Nonstoppers.* The Knows have a self-confidence that shines in situations ranging from the workplace to hanging out with friends to dealing with parents. Some older people describe the Knows' self-confidence as entitlement, arrogance, or overconfidence. Among our generation, the Knows are perceived as having a swagger, self-certainty, or a general sense of confidence. The Whatevers, on the other hand, refuse to bother with the difficulties of life. In tough situations or facing difficult decisions, Whatevers rarely feel it is worth the time or energy to deal with the issues. Finally, the Nonstoppers are compelled to reach goals and take all necessary steps to ensure achievement. They may lose sleep to hit deadlines or continually multitask, but Nonstoppers find a way to reach goals. Yet, Nonstoppers' never experience their goals as fulfilled because there is always more to accomplish. While no single person completely fits into any one category, the three styles provide insight into how our generation responds to the obstacles that arise when striving to realize dreams.

Shortly after the race began, the tortoise's decision about his next move would reflect his style. If he was one of the Knows, the poor start may have damaged his pride to the point that he would rather throw in the towel immediately and save his reputation than potentially face more humiliation. If he was one of the Whatevers, he may have felt that the energy needed to catch up was too overwhelming and the race was not important enough to keep pressing forward. Finally, if the tortoise was a Nonstopper, he may have powered forward despite the gap between him and the hare. While none of these decisions is right or wrong, the Knows or Whatevers definitely would have missed the goal because they would not have continued the race.

What is behind these three styles of managing obstacles? Each style has a different perspective on the meaning of the word "obstacle." The Knows view an obstacle as an indication that they are not capable of reaching the goal or will be embarrassed if they continue to pursue the goal. The Whatevers see the obstacle as an indication that the goal is not worth pursuing. The Nonstoppers acknowledge the obstacle as another hurdle to overcome en route to the goal. Knows and Whatevers expect for the road to be easy, that no obstacles will arise. The Nonstoppers, however, view obstacles as a natural part of the race. Obstacles must be overcome to reach the finish line. Regardless of our personal opinions, these styles represent the lens through which many see the road to reaching dreams, and thus can have a significant impact on the next step when difficult situations arise.

Our generation is frequently described as having high expectations for our lives, but does that mean we expect the road to be easy? If many of us are attempting to achieve more than the generations before us, then will we have *more* obstacles to overcome? Distinguishing between high expectations and a realistic perspective on the necessary steps to reach the goal was important for the tortoise to move pass the first obstacle. While he expected to achieve an almost impossible goal, he had a realistic perspective on what it would take to arrive there.

Do we, as individuals and as a generation, have realistic perspectives about what is necessary to achieve the goals that sprout from high expectations? If we want to travel the world after college, do we have a plan for saving enough money for an extended trip? If we want to start a family in the next couple of years, have we contemplated the kind of job needed to support a family financially and emotionally? Many of us want to become rich, famous, happy, smart, beautiful, and fulfilled, but have we thought about the necessary steps to get these things? When I was a kid, my friends and I wanted to become NBA superstars more than anything else. One day a coach asked me what I was doing to get there. Was I playing on a club team? Was I practicing a couple of hours a day? Was I eating right and staying away from Philly cheese steaks?

Did I go to sleep with a basketball in my bed? If not, then I did not really want to go to the NBA. That day, I realized I'd rather grip a Philly cheese steak than a basketball and did not want to go to the NBA. We may have the big dreams, but do we have realistic perspectives about what it takes to achieve them?

Halfway There

After the tortoise overcame the first major obstacle, the long road towards the finish line lay ahead. Pushing forward in the race was another challenge. Further, his distractions persisted. Despite claiming an early victory over them, he quickly learned that they might take a short break from time to time, but they never completely disappear. Further down the road, the hare was in the thick of the race as well. He had blasted out of the gate to take an early lead and was halfway to the finish line. He figured that his enormous lead had earned him a quick nap. In other words, both the tortoise and the hare were at the midpoint of the race; it's just that the tortoise's midpoint was much closer to the starting line. Each handled this part of the race in very different ways. The tortoise kept moving forward and the hare took a nap. What was behind each of their decisions? How did they go about figuring out the next step?

After we take the first steps toward reaching a goal, the end of the road continues to feel a long way off. The midpoint can be the most difficult part because we exerted so much energy to arrive at that point, yet there is a long road ahead. Frustration can surface when a goal remains unachieved after vigorously working toward it for however many days, weeks, months, or years. We want it to happen now, not later. How do we, as individuals and as a generation, choose to deal with our midpoints?

Our generation has access to technology that makes our lives more convenient than anytime in history. When we're hungry, throwing food in the microwave quickly fills the belly. When we miss a television show and waiting for the rerun takes too long, watching the show online provides a quick solution. When we need a piece of information, a quick search on the computer or cell phone remedies the problem in minutes (if not seconds). Each of these conveniences makes our lives much easier, while building expectations that if we want something then we should have it immediately. The media often supports these expectations. Articles and television specials that profile people who made millions of dollars in what appears to be a very short amount of time provide evidence of quick gratification. Every story of someone getting rich quickly strengthens our belief that we deserve to reach our goals fast.

How does this belief unfold at the midpoint of the race? For Knows, it may take the form of a "nap." After putting forth effort to start the school year right, to have a solid relationship, or to have a good day by keeping a positive attitude, Knows may decide to take a break. Maybe they believe their skills are so sharp that pushing forward is not necessary because the rest of the race will naturally lead to victory. Maybe they believe that their early effort will easily carry them to the finish line. Either way, they decide that nap time has arrived.

For Whatevers, nap time may show the goal is not important enough to sustain a high level of effort. The fatigue and burnout from the initial effort take their toll, and they rethink whether to finish the race. Staying in school and doing the schoolwork, talking about the argument that threatened a solid relationship, or looking past the person who could ruin a great day are too much for Whatevers to handle. Their only solution is taking a nap – a short break that may turn into the deep slumber of quitting.

The Nonstoppers, however, feel that the midpoint is the time to keep moving forward, even if at a tortoise's pace. It's time to complete just thirty minutes of homework if that's all they can tolerate that day. It's necessary to talk after an argument so the relationship will not be jeopardized. Walking away and counting to ten may be the best immediate resolution to the annoying person who might ruin a good mood. It's time to do something, even if it is very small, to keep moving toward the goal.

How do we decide what to do and resist the urge to take a nap? When things start getting difficult, it's natural to try to make the situation easier. Most people strive to become comfortable, not uncomfortable. Yet the road to many of our goals reaches uncomfortable situations that force us to decide whether to push through the discomfort or avoid dealing with it and quit the race. I have a feeling the tortoise had a few tricks up his sleeve (or shell) that helped him keep moving forward despite a difficult road ahead.

The hare probably never considered the tortoise's crafty first trick: to challenge the hare to race in the forest the tortoise called home. The tortoise knew the lay of the land and had a superior understanding of what was needed to reach the finish line. He had the high expectation of winning the race, but the realistic perspective of what it would take. As a result, he probably created a realistic plan for reaching his goal. He knew he needed to get past the first pond within ten minutes, around the big oak tree within thirty minutes, and if he came down the dirt path within the next hour then he was in good shape. His knowledge of the forest, gained through his experiences, gave him the tools he needed to design a plan for reaching the finish line and winning the race against the hare.

When we set our sights on a goal, how do we prepare to realize our dream? Do we jump into the race without thinking about the best strategy? Unprepared, do we become frustrated each time an unexpected obstacle arises? Or do we follow the lead of the tortoise and design a plan that will result in a strong run to the finish line? We might stick to our decision to stay fit if we know that exercising for at least twenty minutes a day for six weeks is necessary to lose ten pounds. Asking a co-worker what steps she took to complete a big project may be key for us to break a project down into manageable tasks and complete it. Plans help keep the race in perspective; we can create mini-goals that give us a specific target to aim at while reaching for the big goal. Author Diana Scharf Hunt described goals as "dreams with deadlines." While the dream may feel like an impossible race to run and win, a plan breaks the goal down into smaller steps that we can walk.

With a plan in place, the tortoise had only one thing to do: *implement* the plan. It doesn't make sense to go through the trouble of making a plan and then do something else. The tortoise then pulled the second trick out of his bag: discipline. Often, discipline is used on misbehaving kids who need a timeout. On the racetrack, however, discipline is the magic that moves us from the starting line to the finish line. Discipline is magical in its ability to breathe life into a plan. The plan alone would not have done much for the tortoise, but sticking to the plan did. He stuck to the plan during beautiful sunshine and when it started to rain. He stuck to the plan when he had a clear path and when there were sticks in the way that made it difficult to move forward. He stuck to the plan when he felt like it and when he did not. Sticking with the plan moved the tortoise past the hare as he snoozed under a shade tree.

How do we exert discipline in our lives while running our individual races? Is studying for a few minutes after leaving the job each day an option to keep up in classes? Will taking a few more hours during the week ensure a quality presentation? Do we schedule time for that special person on a regular basis and keep our dates? As individuals and as a generation, do we do what's necessary to reach our goals even when we don't feel like it? Do we have discipline? We can try to answer with words, but once the race is over, they are answered by actions. Motivational speaker Jim Rohn observed that "we must all suffer from one of two pains: the pain of discipline or the pain of regret. The difference is discipline weighs ounces while regret weighs tons."

The magic of discipline is that it gives legs to plans and helps us move closer to the big goal, even if we're moving at a tortoise's pace. Sometimes the little tasks done in the name of discipline feel like drops of water in an ocean. It seems we complete task after task without seeing any results. Yet something is happening that is easy to overlook. A student learns a new concept that accounts for only one question on the midterm, but is necessary for understanding two or three other concepts that will be on the test. A woman training for a fifteen-mile race can run two miles as opposed to the one mile she was running last week. This is a job seeker's sixth networking event this month and he is just meeting someone who may have a job he is interested in. While all the work completed to that point may feel insufficient, it's giving the person something to build on to move closer to the finish line. In time, it becomes easier to understand about half the concepts for the midterm, seven miles is run with ease, and a new job offer is evidence that the networking events were not in vain. In "What It Takes to Be Great," an October 19, 2006, article in *Fortune* magazine, Geoffrey Colvin found no evidence that natural talent is the biggest contributor to great success. Instead, he reported that demanding practice and hard work

were consistently the foundation of all extraordinary achievement. The magic of discipline is that all the little tasks done
over time accumulate and become one big accomplishment.

While planning takes time and following through takes
effort, I wonder what was on the tortoise's mind once he had a
plan in place and decided to follow through. He probably had
a lot of time to think. He probably had plenty of opportunities
to let the distractions return and fill his head with reasons why
he should still quit the race. How did he keep those thoughts
and feelings from making him quit? He may have tried to
avoid thinking about the animals that said he could not make it
or entertaining the lingering doubts in his heart about his ability to win the race. The problem with this strategy is that
trying not to think about something can make us think about it
even more. So as opposed to freeing himself of the negative
thoughts and feelings, he probably had to replace them with
something that would help him continue toward the finish
line.

To keep himself motivated to continue the race, the tortoise probably pulled his third trick out of the bag:
mindfulness. Mindfulness can have an enormous impact on
how we stay motivated to achieve a goal. It refers to an awareness and appreciation of what we are experiencing at this
moment. Mindfulness means letting go of the regrets of the
past and nervousness for the future and instead focusing on
the moment at hand. Mindfulness also challenges a person to
appreciate that experience. The tortoise could have dwelled

on his poor start to the race or fretted over the long road ahead of him. However, I have a feeling that he took this long walk as an opportunity to feel the warm sun on his shell as he moved his legs as fast as humanly (or turtlely) possible. He probably smelled the fresh flowers budding by the maple tree and enjoyed the downhill stretches that gave him a chance to slide upside down on his shell while giggling to himself and feeling the breeze on his cheeks. Every little thing that was happening gave him an opportunity to appreciate the surrounding world and truly enjoy the race as opposed to dreading each obstacle he might face.

How do we deal with our thoughts when we are racing toward our goals? Are we consumed by regrets? Do we obsess on uncontrollable aspects of the race? Or do we appreciate the journey as the dream becomes a reality? Our generation is often asked what grade we got on the test, how much the boss liked our project, or whether we got the promotion. While there is nothing wrong with these questions, each focuses on the end product and not the ongoing process. Being bombarded with such questions can cause us to lose sight of the little treats we gain along the way. The experiences we have while working toward a goal are rich and full of opportunities to appreciate the world around us, yet are frequently overlooked in favor of the end goal. Nonstoppers are particularly susceptible to this tendency. In a chase to acquire the degree, achieve the promotion, or start a committed relationship, they may forget to notice how interesting learning is, what a joy it is to go into work every day, or the person who first captured their heart. Eckhart Tolle, philosopher and author of *A New Earth,* suggests that during our search to reach life goals we each need to "realize deeply that the present moment is all you ever have." It is easy to believe that tomorrow holds all the good fortune or memories are the only possession worth cherishing, but each time we slow ourselves down mentally to appreciate the present moment and the process, it usually gives us a little more energy to push forward.

While managing the mind is one half of the challenge to stay motivated during the thick of the race, managing attitudes and feelings is the other half. During the race, the tortoise probably had moments in which he felt tired, frustrated about the road ahead, or upset that he was in the race at all. These feelings may have built up to the point that he just wanted to get the race over with, regardless of how it ended. How did the tortoise move beyond these feelings and stay motivated? It probably called for him to pull one last trick out of his bag: the right attitude. At first this trick may seem vague and difficult to make happen in tough situations. Yet the tortoise had complete control over his attitude and so it was one of the least difficult tricks to pull off.

Part of the right attitude is optimism and hope in the face of adversity. While obstacles are bound to exist, the way we react to those obstacles is often in our control. The tortoise could choose to see the rocks on the path or the stretches of road without shade from the sun as reasons to question why he was racing and become upset for challenging the hare. Or, he could see the rocks and the lack of shade as temporary hardships that would place him closer to an unbelievable goal. His outlook, or attitude, toward such challenges probably influenced whether he decided to keep moving forward or throw in the towel early.

The right attitude also involves choosing urgency over rushing. To rush would be to speed through the race as quickly as possible regardless of how that happens; to take an attitude of urgency would be to plan the best strategy for reaching the finish line and complete the race as quickly as possible. Rushing may mean speeding off at the beginning and taking a nap while the race is still in the balance. Rushing may have caused the hare to make mistakes that he could have avoided if he slowed down and planned better. Rushing usually leads to actions that are not helpful for reaching the goal. An attitude of urgency, on the other hand, is to be aware of how important it is to win the race, but with the acknowledgment that a plan must be designed and followed. In essence, urgency means being patient when it is time to be patient and decisive when it is time to be decisive. Maybe the tortoise scheduled two-minute breaks to ensure he had the energy to maintain a steady pace. Maybe he designed a plan that prepared him to speed up at some points in the race and slowing down in others. The attitude of urgency guided the tortoise to make decisions that placed him in the best position to reach the finish line and win the race.

How do our attitudes impact our chances of achieving the goal? The temptation to rush is always present because it seems like the quick way to achieve the dream. Finishing school is the top priority so schoolwork of any quality is acceptable simply to pass the class. A project at work is becoming increasingly annoying, so the easy fix is to ask someone else to finish it without checking to see if the person is capable of doing the project correctly. Being in a relationship is such a burning desire that a woman dates a married man. While rushing may give a brief feeling of accomplishment, the shortcuts taken usually make the achievement less gratifying. The person graduated from college, but without grades good enough to land a decent job. The project was completed, but the poor quality caused the boss to see the employee in a less favorable light. She has a relationship, but it is a dead end.

An attitude of urgency has us think through how to reach goals and avoid the pitfalls. It inspires planning for the inevitable obstacles, while acknowledging the importance of reaching the goal as soon as possible. It helps us maintain the optimistic and hopeful attitude we need to move forward.

Victory Line

As the tortoise turned the corner and began the home stretch toward the finish line, I can imagine the excitement and astonishment in the air. The same tortoises that warned him about ruining his reputation and their reputations cheered him with pride. The birds that advised him not to run the race because the course was difficult hovered over the finish line, impressed with this improbable victory. The fish that laughed looked confused and amazed that the tortoise actually pulled it off. As the tortoise approached the finish line, the cheers became progressively louder. He was tired, but he knew he was too close to give up now. His goal was in sight. He was running on adrenaline. *Three trees to go*, he probably thought. As the tortoise began his countdown to victory, the hare was waking to the cheers of the forest. Not sure how long he had been asleep, the hare bolted up and zoomed down the road. *Two trees to go*, the tortoise whispered to himself. The cheers were getting louder. *That tortoise can't be anywhere near the finish line yet?!?* the hare thought. *One more tree and then victory.* The hare was panicking now. *There is no way!!!* the hare said as he turned the corner and saw the crowd cheering the tortoise on to the finish line. *One more step* the tortoise said to himself as he stepped over the finish line. Victory! The tortoise had done the impossible: he won the race against the hare.

The poor start of the race and the struggles during the thick of it became distant memories, and all the tortoise and the rest of the forest knew was that the tortoise won. Further, the tortoise's victory involved finishing *well*. Finishing well is not just crossing the finish line, but crossing the finish line in a race well run. And a race well run is marked by persistence, smart decisions, and self-improvement. This is victory.

We have all witnessed someone who had big dreams and started with much promise but never reached his potential. His grades were great. He earned the internship to keep moving up the career ladder. He was on track to realize all of his goals. Then the internship was cut due to funding restraints and his grades were steadily declining. He decided to pursue a less challenging career because the work to realize the original dream was too difficult. He slowly became unrecognizable. All that remained were memories of an early effort and an unfulfilled dream. Unrealized dreams and goals are difficult to recover from and can become the start of a pattern. Others lose faith, but more importantly, we lose faith. Finishing well in the present gives us confidence to finish well in the future.

While the tortoise used his discipline, mindset, attitude, and feelings to persevere, there was still something else. What? Whereas the hare ran for his personal glory and to add another notch to his belt, the tortoise had much more at stake than his reputation. He carried the hopes of the forest on his back. If he pulled off this victory then other tortoises could walk with boldness around the forest without fear of ridicule by the hare. Other different animals might develop greater mutual respect and come to a more peaceful coexistence. When the tortoise was the victor, the forest animals' beliefs about the potential of each creature were drastically expanded. A loss for the tortoise would have been a loss for the forest because his goal was much bigger than himself.

Why does each of us reach for our dreams? *Why* do we push for our goals? Figuring out *why* is difficult, particularly when talking about personal goals and dreams, yet may light the spark we need to push forward when everything and everyone around is yelling, "Turn back!" When I was in college, I needed a flexible job that allowed me to pay the bills and gave me time to study. I joined a network marketing company. Network marketing is a way to sell goods directly to customers and receive a commission based on the amount of merchandise sold. It sounded easy enough. What I didn't realize was this job would turn me into a nonstop salesman. After a while, I became the guy who caused everyone to say, "Oh gosh, here he comes to sell me some more stuff!" With that reputation, it's easy to understand why I received many more refusals than orders for knives, telephone service, plane tickets, and .... (If you can think of it, I probably sold it.) With rejection so plentiful, it was easy to become discouraged.

Time after time I wanted to quit, but I stayed committed. While I would like to take full credit for that, it was the training I received before I even approached my first potential customer that gave me the fortitude to withstand so much rejection. In the training session, I was asked why I was doing this. I replied quickly with reasons like "I want to make money" and "it's flexible so I can keep up with my studies." Each answer I gave was countered by the trainers with, "Is that really the only reason why you chose to do *this* business?". Network marketing was a tough business, but I didn't think it was anything extraordinary. Then the trainers walked me through the possibilities of becoming financially free and having complete control over my time. They broadened my perspective and in the process broadened my thinking about *why* I decided to do the business. I began telling them that my reasons were to pay for my parents' retirement, to earn enough so my future family and spouse did not need to work, and to spend time working in the community without worrying about paying bills. It was at that moment they told me that my *why* was big enough and I was ready to face the tough road ahead.

I asked earlier in this chapter whether the story of the tortoise and the hare is relevant to our generation. I wondered whether moving persistently toward our goals could coexist with our generation's focus on finding something we are passionate about. The answer came when the tortoise let his *why* become big enough. At some point (I don't know which), the race became about much more than the tortoise trying to beat the hare. For the hare, the race was about remaining the king of the forest and the result was that a nap cost him the race and the title. His *why* was not big enough. At first the tortoise was simply tired of the hare's teasing, but at some point, I have a feeling the tortoise looked around the forest and saw baby tortoises peeking at him, saw the birds above shaking their heads in disappointment at the prospect of another win for the hare, and felt the slight nervous excitement in his stomach that signaled the possibility of something great. It would be at this moment that the tortoise received the drive, the *why*, the passion that was big enough to fuel him through the race.

The tortoise needed to get beyond himself. For me to keep selling to people knowing I would get rejected 95% of the time, I had to get beyond myself.

Our goals and dreams begin as small seeds deep within us that grow into ideas about who we have the potential to become and what we have the potential to achieve. In themselves, these seeds are without the strength or passion to survive the hard times. It is only when they grow and connect with something bigger than ourselves that they stand a chance. It is this passion that drives someone who dreams of becoming a doctor to see beyond the years of medical school and student loans to the moment she will help people live healthier, longer lives. It is this burning desire that pushes a guy to embrace his longtime girlfriend after a hurtful fight because he understands that the life they are building together is beautiful and special. Moving beyond ourselves fuels the endurance to cross the finish line.

Long after the race was finished, one thing remained: the victory. The legacy left by the victory of the tortoise resonated through the forest long after the celebrations stopped. It gave the baby tortoises a model for becoming bold older tortoises. It gave the fish a reason to respect all animals because they knew they could not predict what any animal was capable of. It gave the birds courage to fly a little bit further to bring food back to their nests. This one small victory from this one little tortoise sparked a change in the forest that no one had seen before.

In *The Tipping Point*, Malcolm Gladwell outlines example after example in which one small change by a person sparked a change in the world so massive that others were forced to change their ways. In essence, he argues that the smallest action by a person has the potential to shift a situation in such a drastic way that change in others is inevitable. We have this potential, but do we dream big enough? Do we plan well enough? Do we get beyond ourselves often enough? Do we listen when inspired, and, if we do listen, do we follow through? Will we, as individuals and as a generation, spark meaningful change through our goals and dreams?

Interlude:
Boxes

Time to pack ...
There is so much stuff everywhere,
I already have half of everything packed in these boxes and
there is so much stuff left.
Where do I even begin?!?
Well I was told to put everything that is the same together so
that I can easily find it.
You know, you don't want to be looking for your toothbrush in
the bathroom box and come to find out it was lying by your
baseball cards in your "stuff she wants me to throw away" box.
Well let's see what we have here ...

Here's the career box. It used to say dreams, but I had to cross
that out because they told me that its name didn't match the
box it was suppose to go into. Once the name was changed it
only fit into the office box. This is the first time I have ever
brought the office box home because it's not even mine. I
don't own it and the owner told me that it couldn't come home.
But the thing that gets me is that I can't leave the box "unat-
tended." At least that's what the owner said. So I am almost
always with the office box, but the office box is always in the
office (who would've guessed). So guess where I usually am ...
To think, I collected all those school boxes just to end up with
that one big office box. I mean I had the nicest school boxes
too! They were ivy colored and everything. Yet, all I ended up
doing is babysitting an office box eight to ten hours a day (ele-
ven hours if you include the time I travel), getting a lunchbox
for thirty minutes of that eight to ten hours, and spending
maybe an hour or two with my family box.

Speaking of the family box, there is all this family stuff. I may
need a couple of boxes for this. I never could find my father so
I was told the only box my family will fit in is the dysfunctional
box. Instead of putting my whole family in the dysfunctional
box, I just put my sister in there because she said that she
doesn't want to get married. She's satisfied with the life she
has and feels fulfilled. So I am told that she is definitely a

product of a dysfunctional box and should be placed where she belongs. Since I decided (I think I decided) to collect nice school boxes, get a big office box, and live the rest of my life with a box that was the same color as my family box, I was told that I don't have to be in the dysfunctional family box. I can have a normal family box. Not only that, my own parents gave me a good life box because of all these nice boxes I've collected. Over there are the people boxes. There are so many of them. Some of them I know; some I don't. Some are friends and others are not.

I'm shipping this box to Thailand; this box goes to India.
This box right here is going to Compton.
That bright yellow box right there, I'm sending it by train to the East.

I was told that the best way to know where to put people is to color code the boxes and put all the people in them accordingly. Some of my friends are in the black box, but to me it seems like some of them would better fit in the white box, but then again I'm supposed to keep things organized. So that means no mixing and matching. I don't know how my black box got so beat up?!? I guess since I let my boss borrow it for the past couple of years and he probably just put it in a dirty room where it started to corrode. He probably figured since it was black, no one would see the dirt. Well I do. I thought the white box was clean, but I had one of those gadgets that let's you see dirt in the dark. So I turned off the lights and used it to see how clean my boxes really were. You know what ... the white box is just as dirty as all the other boxes. Ha, my boss could've fooled me! I let him borrow the white box and it looked like it was so clean when he brought it back. He said that he kept it on a high shelf so it wouldn't get dirty from the floor. So I have these brown boxes that are going to Mexico and all these other little boxes that are going to the Middle East. I'm told that those little boxes headed toward the Middle East are going to take a little longer to arrive at their destination because extra security measures are in place when those boxes travel.

So, I have the office box, the family boxes, the people boxes ... what's left? I think that's it. It's funny, when I was younger and we were moving there was so much stuff all over the place. I was always playing with everything not thinking twice about if I'm taking it out of order. It was my parents and their parents who told me everything has to be kept in order. Well, come to think of it, I remember my teachers saying that everything had to be kept in order. Hold on, I remember people at my church saying that quite a bit too! Yeah, I remember seeing it on TV a lot too. Come to think of it, just about everyone I've ever known has told me that things have to be kept in order and properly placed in their boxes. What would happen if I don't put it in a box? What's so great about these boxes anyway!?! Why am I moving in the first place? I like where I live! I like having my things all over the place!!! I don't mind taking a little bit more time to find what I am looking for. Besides, it was more fun when I was kid ... before I even knew what a box was.

Chapter 5:
Interdependence

"We are caught in an inescapable network of mutuality, tied in a single garment of destiny."

~ Martin Luther King, Jr.

"Hey, what r u up 2?" Tom texted Christine. Christine looked at her phone and knew she shouldn't respond. Her friends said they saw Tom going to the movies with Angela last week. Christine decided to play it cool and texted back "nothing much." On the other end, Tom thought carefully about the next text. According to her profile page, Christine had just become single. Tom didn't want to come off as if he were trying to catch her on the rebound. Even though most people thought Tom never kept a woman around too long, he actually liked Christine a lot. Ever since the first time he saw her at school a few months ago, he wanted to get to know her. Playing it smart he texted back, "just wanted to see how you are ... free to talk?" Christine thought about it for a little while. Part of her did not want him to take advantage of her, like he did with all the other women she heard about. Yet part of her felt that Tom sincerely wanted to get to know her – and she wanted to get to know him, too. As thoughts of all the possible outcomes of her next decision raced through Christine's head, her fingers typed "sure."

For most of us, our relationships are our most prized possessions. We treasure a warm conversation with Mom, the hilarious comment from a best friend, and the pure joy of being in the presence of that special person. Such encounters show human beings in the unique position of having meaningful relationships, characterized by one person deeply influencing another. Yet, underlying this treasure of human experience is a constant tug-of-war. For most people, an internal debate often brews about how close to draw to another person, how vulnerable to become, or whether it is even worth the time and energy to invest in a relationship. As Tom's and Christine's exchange suggests, the future of our relationships is uncertain, so we tend to tread cautiously. Most of us are lured in by the possibility of fulfilling some aspect of ourselves personally with each interaction, but are well aware of the potential danger if a relationship goes wrong. Whether relationships are familial, friendly, professional, or romantic, we strive to balance our desire to exist as distinct individuals, independent of others, with our natural longing to reap the benefits of relating to other people.

Achieving this balance is an ongoing challenge throughout our lives, beginning as early as we can talk and enduring until we die. It is driven by one of the most fundamental questions of the human journey: how do we connect with others? Many of us wonder what others think about us, read situations before we act to avoid awkwardness, and have a range of emotional responses to what others do (or do not do) to us. We are attempting to navigate a world that requires us to interact with other people. In our minds, through our actions, and with our feelings, we are constantly trying to figure out where our distinctions as individuals end and the connections with other people begin. The boundary we create often decides how we treat others and, ultimately, how we think about ourselves in relation to the rest of the world. With this in mind, a fundamental question: how do we, as individuals and as a generation, connect to others today, and why is our connection (or lack of connection) important?

Connection Stages

When an infant first enters this world, she makes her first connection with others. Crying, screaming, and flailing her little arms and legs, she shows the world that she has one way to connect: through dependence. She depends on others to feed her, to keep warm, to feel better when she is upset. Her dependence on others is not a choice but necessary for her survival. What happens when a newborn baby does not have the food, clothing, or shelter she needs to protect her? She fails to thrive, or worse. And beyond her physical needs, forming an emotional bond with someone early in life is also crucial to how she develops. When a baby builds a strong positive emotional bond with her caretaker then it is much more likely that she becomes a person with high self-esteem, a happy disposition, and healthy relationships. Clearly, a lot happens before the baby can say a word and, more importantly, before she can do anything for herself.

As she develops, she begins to see the world through a slightly different lens. She realizes her little legs can take her places that her parents did not tell her to go. She notices her hands can grab objects without help. She understands that despite depending on others for many things, she can complete many tasks without anyone's help. She learns the second way we connect with others: independence.

Unlike the one-way interaction of dependence, independence allows us to create some distance from others. At first she wants to do simple things independently, like walk alone across the room instead of being carried. As she grows older, it becomes a little more complex and she wants to make her lunch without her parents' help or ride her bike to a friend's house as opposed to her parents driving her. Then she becomes a teenager and wants to start buying the clothes that she prefers and spending time with the friends she likes. She wants to become independent from people who try to tell her what she should or should not do. She wants to understand the world for herself. We all disconnect from others by trying to show them (and often ourselves) that we have the ability to do things on our own.

Yet with each attempt at independence, there are constant reminders that eventually we need another person's help. A teenager may buy the clothes she wants, but the money may have come from her parents. If the money came from a job, then she needed someone to hire her. Whether directly or indirectly, it becomes increasingly clear that dependence on others is never completely eliminated.

Does this dynamic mean that we depend on others in order to gain the strength and resources to be independent? If this is the case, then it points to the third (and less frequently acknowledged) form of connection: interdependence. Interdependence is a mutual dependence that allows each person to gain the most from independence. Unlike the clear one-sided relationships created by dependence and the obvious disconnect that independence creates, interdependence involves a little work from everyone to create a balance of independence and dependence within each person. Interdependence may take more work to understand and to manage where we end and connection with another begins, but the potential payoff is that each person gains the most satisfying life possible. Is interdependence worth it?

Mind Reading

How do people generally figure out with whom to connect in everyday life? Christine and Tom formed strong opinions about each other based on a little bit of information – Christine from her friends and Tom from Christine's profile. Their minds work like every other human's, using the little information gathered from people and situations to form beliefs, opinions, and attitudes about others. While the human brain is extraordinary, it has its limits. Each of us has to make decision after decision simply to progress through the day. We do not always have time to gather all the information we might want to completely assess others. We cannot take hours to figure out what each person is about if we're going to complete the group research paper, collaborate on a business proposal, or simply take the bus home. Quick decisions are needed and limited information is used to decide who is in the group, which colleague to collaborate with, or who to sit beside on the trip home. This quick way of categorizing others helps us move through the day with our sanity intact.

Categorizing others is a natural strategy our minds use to deal with all the information that we are bombarded with every day efficiently and quickly. While nothing is inherently wrong with this process, quickly categorizing people can have its drawbacks. Information that's missing might be very helpful. What if Tom's "date" to the movies was his cousin? That information would have helped Christine form a more accurate opinion of Tom. One of the biggest drawbacks of how our minds work is our tendency to place people into categories even if we do not have enough information to be accurate.

We receive information about what to think of others and how best to navigate the world from friends, family, television, the Internet, experiences, teachers, churches, and other sources. Parents tell their children not to hang out with "those kind of people" because they are "bad." Friends tell their buddy that a group of kids is cool because they have money. The media's perspectives often fuel stereotypes. Some of the information is helpful in forming an accurate view of people, while other information is inaccurate. Regardless, the information is always limited and we use it to form quick opinions of others.

Where do these quickly formed opinions lead? They usually lead us to place people into one of two categories: like us or not like us. The "us" is not necessarily a group of people, but a group of characteristics that we deem important and that represent who we are. If the point of gathering information is to navigate the world better, it's natural to gravitate toward the familiar and to be wary of the unfamiliar. When we see something in other people that we recognize, something familiar, we feel a little more comfortable because we know what to expect. We think about how our family is kind of like his or how she seems interested in the same stuff that we are. Every step closer to familiarity puts each person more at ease. We naturally believe it is easier to connect with other people when they are like us.

What about people who are not like us? How do we handle them? Often, we are cautious. Differences may manifest through gender, race, class, or another quality. Regardless, we do not know what to expect, so we naturally make every effort to avoid a situation that can potentially jeopardize personal safety. Each of us wants to protect our financial future, look out for our families, and ensure personal emotional security. We are cautious about those who are not like us because we are concerned that in some way they will make us less safe. As we learn more about them, our concerns can grow and cautiousness can transform into fear. Our fear is not just that a relationship might jeopardize personal safety, but that we feel the other is actively trying to disassemble our safe haven.

Once we feel threatened in this way, we make every effort to avoid contact. This fear pushes us to do whatever it takes for protection.

We fear those who are not like us because we do not see anything in them that is like us. We believe that the things that make us happy, the situations that make us worry, or the dreams that we have for our lives do not have anything in common with those who are not like us. This makes it easy to believe that those who are not like us will take care of themselves even if it means that we must suffer. Since there are only so many resources, someone has to suffer, right? Everyone cannot have high-paying jobs or the demand declines and the jobs are no longer valuable. Only certain people can have control of the world; otherwise, there is no order. There are only so many resources and everyone wants to protect what they believe rightly belongs to them, right?

With this perspective, something else begins to bubble to the surface after fear has taken root. We become upset that self-protection is necessary. We start feeling that those who are not like us have no right to the same resources as us because we have worked our whole lives to earn what we have. The seeds of hate are planted. Hate drives us to lump all the people we feel threaten us into one category. When hate comes into the picture, we strip those who are not like us down to the point that they are nothing more than the reason we hate them. They are no longer human. They are the people who are trying to take our jobs. They are the women who should not be in leadership positions because of their gender. They are the men who belong in that neighborhood and no-where else. They are individuals who do not deserve connection with anyone, and so disconnection becomes the solution. Separate but equal, gender bias, racial discrimina-tion, and prejudice become tools to make that disconnect as permanent as possible. Sometimes these disconnects are overt, when we make it clear that certain types of people are not wanted in our schools, neighborhoods, circle of friends, or jobs. Other times it is less obvious and we find "polite" ways to inform people that they are not wanted. A gentle rebuff stating that he is not qualified for the job when he actually is, a sug-gestion for her to connect with others who she may like better, or a sarcastic quip about someone's accent is a below-the-radar attempt to separate ourselves from certain types of people – people who are not like us.

These are age-old issues, but how is our generation handling them? While those before us dealt with them as well, there was one tool they did not have to help navigate their world: the Internet. The Internet has revolutionized the way that we connect. E-mail enables us to communicate around the world in seconds. We can research any topic from our desks – or a coffee shop. We use social networks to check on our friends' every move. We read or watch the latest news on the computer – even if it is happening halfway around the world at that very moment. The Internet has given us opportunities to connect in ways that humans have never connected before, while also providing a tool to help us figure out life.

Many have suggested that the Internet has made our world much smaller. Hailed as a man before his time, Canadian professor of communications and philosopher Marshall McLuhan created the term "global village" to describe how electronic technology fundamentally changed the world. While many of his ideas focused on the impact of television in the 1960s, his idea that the world becomes smaller when people receive information from around the world in a matter of seconds has had staying power. The quickness with which information flows today has given many people reason to believe that our generation's concept of connection to others has completely shifted from generations before us.

One of the major shifts is the increased *need* for our generation to connect with others. Technology allows us to text someone from class, post pictures from a crazy night out, or read a blog just posted about another movie a friend does not like. With all of the ways to connect, we have more ways to retrieve information about others and more chances to express ourselves and display our individuality in every facet of life.

While the avenues for connection have increased, many wonder whether the *quality* of connections has decreased. Many of us talk on the phone, chat via instant messenger, send quick messages through e-mail and text, and do everything in our power to avoid face-to-face contact. With the ease of connecting electronically, are we avoiding in-person contact and the opportunities it provides to gain information face to face? If information is the key to deciding whether others are like us or not like us, then is it possible that the way we connect as a generation is a double-edge sword? On one hand, we can gather information about others that may lead to a more accurate understanding of who that person is. On the other, if the information is false or loses some of its clarity each time it is conveyed by text, e-mail, status update, or other speedy electronic method, is what we're receiving less accurate? The adage "a picture's worth a thousand words" speaks to the notion that experiencing a person in person is much more revealing than any verbal description. Are we losing sight of the big picture?

Balancing Act

As we become more aware of *what* connects us, the big picture for *how* we connect becomes clearer. As Tom and Christine embarked upon their romantic journey, they spent time talking about their favorite movies, cool places to hang out, and the people in their lives. Some aspect of their families' beliefs crept into the discussion. Whether it was how Tom's mom never cared for his friends from the 'hood or how Christine's father always teased about her bleeding heart for anyone who could breathe, each realized that their perspectives on the world were considerably different than their parents'.

In many ways, our generation's way of viewing others and thinking about differences has shifted. Many of us show a greater appreciation for the diversity embedded in our communities, society, and circle of friends. We want people to take pride in who they are and express themselves freely. The Internet is a perfect outlet for us to express our individuality, while keeping those we don't care for distant.

Despite the tools our generation has to connect, these tools also create opportunities for disconnection. Someone can upload a profile picture that indicates his religious beliefs, and others can leave unpleasant or disrespectful comments on the page. A woman can submit her resume for a job she is qualified to do and position her cultural background as an asset, but the company may reject her application with a generic reply that leaves her believing that her gender or cultural background was not welcome. These disconnections are the same prejudices and biases of previous generations at work through different tools. The Internet can be a tool for confirming fears and "justifying" hatred, both of which serve the same purpose discussed earlier: to protect. Hate and fear serve to protect connections with the "right" people and to keep resources from being stolen by those who are different.

Is our generation seeking to understand how discrimination and prejudice against one group affects everyone else? What is the greater impact if she does not get that job because she is a woman and he can't live in that neighborhood because of the color of his skin? We routinely interact with others who are different. We work with people who do not seem like us. We are in classes with people we do not understand. Our groceries, clothes, and technology are often manufactured by people we believe have nothing to do with us. Yet the Internet pulls us closer together in unprecedented ways. We can watch a video clip online while someone thousands of miles away watches the same clip and laughs at the same joke. The tension between differences and the concept of the global village remains one of the chief concerns of the human experience: how we balance our dependence on others with a satisfying sense of independence.

This balancing act resembles the high-wire performances of circus entertainers. Each of us wants to keep our balance on the tightrope between independence and dependence. Yet people who are not like us seem ever present and ready to disturb that balance. They take the valued jobs, get the promotion, or receive the graduate school offer, seemingly leaving fewer chances for us to achieve a satisfying independent life. In some way, it makes sense to protect ourselves from these "others."

But is there a risk to protecting ourselves from those who are not like us? If we're constantly thinking about how to avoid losing our balance because of others, does that slow us down as we walk the tightrope? Does it stop us from enjoying what we already have? If our forward movement is cautious and we don't feel any joy because of our constant fear of losing our balance, then is the journey worth it? These questions are relevant to our attempts to find the right people to support the independent lives we want to create. The solution can seem to lie in limiting our interactions with people who are not like us.

Martin Luther King, Jr., said "An injustice anywhere is a threat to justice everywhere." He believed that there is something deeper than how a person looks on the outside that ties us together as humans. This was not a novel concept. For centuries, philosophers and scholars have observed aspects of the human experience that are common among people regardless of their backgrounds. In the early 1900s, psychiatrist and philosopher Carl Jung went as far as suggesting that humans have a collective unconscious. He believed that underlying each person's conscious awareness is a common way of seeing the world that leads every culture to ideas about what it means to have a family, assign roles in society, and become a man or a woman. While the ideas may look different in different cultures, Jung was convinced that there is an aspect of every human being that is tied to everyone else.

The belief in commonality within the human experience continues through media, literature, and the rhetoric of many modern leaders. Movies like *Crash* and *Babel* highlight how people from very different backgrounds have many of the same goals and desires. People want to live in safe neighborhoods with their families. People want to have enough money to care for themselves and others in their close circles. People want to find love. With more exchange of information than at any other time in history, news of people struck by tragedy is constant – and resonates because most people can relate. The

Internet can unearth information that helps us realize that "they" are actually like us in many ways.

With this understanding, is it possible that our human commonality makes acknowledging our interdependence the solution for maintaining our balance on the tightrope? One of the most brilliant minds of the twentieth century, Albert Einstein, observed, "A hundred times a day I remind myself that my inner and outer life depends on the labor of other [people], living and dead, and that I must exert myself in order to give in the same measure as I have received and am still receiving." His thoughts echoed the sentiments of another great leader, Mahatma Gandhi, who asserted that "interdependence is and ought to be as much the ideal of man as self-sufficiency. Man is a social being." These great leaders believed our survival as individuals depended on whether we understood how to connect in an interdependent manner.

It is difficult to look beyond our individual balancing acts to understand how everyone's balance impacts everyone else. The weight of prejudice or discrimination might keep one person off balance, thus affecting others, if only just a little bit. The fear of connecting with others might nearly paralyze another person on his tightrope; he doesn't move too far from the small segment that feels safe.

When psychologists have looked at how people break through barriers to connection like prejudice and racism, they often come to the conclusion that people have to see the value of others in their lives before they surrender the ideas and beliefs that are obstacles to understanding the benefits of interdependence. To see if this really is the case, psychologist Elliot Aronson did an experiment with a classroom of kids from different racial groups. Most of the kids in the class separated into their respective racial groups without thinking much about it. Since the kids' school had recently desegregated, suspicion and fear led to fights between groups and a general atmosphere of tension in the classroom.

To see if he could change this dynamic, Aronson introduced the "jigsaw classroom." The idea was to create small groups of students of different races and assign each group a big task that was kind of like a puzzle. The big task required completion of many little tasks. Each student was responsible for one little task and had to work with the other kids in the group to ensure the big task was completed. The findings were astounding: kids from different racial groups developed a new respect for each other and a desire to work together in the future.

The whole atmosphere of the classroom changed. Why? After repeating this experiment many times with different people, Aronson concluded that once people work with others who add something valuable to their lives, there is a new willingness to work with them in the future. Whether the willingness comes from a new inclination to see "them" as more like "us" or an understanding that "they" will help "us" reach our goals, a new way of connecting was experienced: interdependence.

Embracing interdependence seems to allow for the meaningful connections that will enable us to balance on our tightropes. In fact, the payoff may be a balance that is difficult to disturb because it brings a sense of satisfaction to life. We get the right amount of support to move forward in life, while enjoying the confidence that we are capable of contributing something unique and worthwhile to the world. When we are in balance, it is easy to see that the resources needed to live a fulfilling life are readily available. We realize that we are so closely tied to others that our tightropes form a net to catch us if we fall. We can start to feel at ease and open ourselves to a pervasive sense of peace when we acknowledge that our connection to others supports our balance rather than disturbs it.

As the world shrinks, we deal with people who do not seem like us more and more, and these dealings can either help or hurt us as we try to find the balance between independence and our need (whether we like it or not) to depend on others. The way to feel ease about those around us is to see them as like us in some way. This is one of few avenues for us to embrace the type of connection that is of utmost importance: interdependence. When the dust of the day settles, is our generation going to let fear continue the disconnections of the past or instead declare a turning point?

Interlude:
Race

We have to pick up the pace.
I know this may not be the time or place.
It's just these problems of class, sex, and race
That make me want to make a case
For the urgency needed to address these issues we face.
We're kidding ourselves if we think we're safe.
Generations before had their battles to fight,
But for us it's even scarier ...
Talk about fight or flight!
The transgression of apathy could turn our days into night.
Then there'll be no need for sight,
Because the horrors of indifference will strike
US OUT!

Then what will there be to see?
Other than the cries and pleas
Of our children and grandchildren asking "why, oh why
Didn't you do anything to change the social climate we live in?
We still suffer from the same vices that are at best repugnant!
There is still no shame for how we treat others because of the
shade of their skin,
Or because their lifestyle does not afford them a zip code from
the Hamptons,
Or just because they have different beliefs, we hate the sinner
and not the sin.
We still refuse to understand the beauty within.
You thought if you sat back and watched
It would wipe out the blotch of hate, greed, and envy
That was cleverly guised in a 'democratic' society.
Yet, apathy became the monarchy.
And the race we run places us further down the path you
created
While bringing our country closer to an unthinkable final
destination:
Internal disintegration and eventually complete annihilation!"

So now where do we stand?
Where do we go to retreat from our past inaction's reprimands?
The answers lie right here … in our hands.
Hands that can hug,
Hands that move the heart with a tug.
Hands that can get dirty with the mud
Of "politically incorrect" conversations
Or simply to refuse the media's propaganda statements,
Or maybe to become the trailblazer for a new path in this race
– A race for equal opportunity for each person in every neighborhood, city, and state
And the development of the America we purport we're trying to shape.

I guess what I'm trying to say
Is that the race will never go away.
The course we run may change,
The weather could be sunny or it may rain.
But regardless of the condition of the course,
We are each runners, either voluntarily or by force.
And since each of us has a stake in this race
It is incumbent upon us to stand face to face
With the divisiveness that surrounds issues such as class and race.
We must hold each other accountable for the decisions we make,
Because it's our children and their children's lives that are at stake.
And I would hate to be responsible for the gravest mistake
Of letting my hands remain idle as my feet run on a course I did not want to take
When change is what my hands had the chance to activate
And now this burden is borne by my namesake.

Chapter 6:
Steps

"Only as high as I reach can I grow, only as far as I seek can I go, only as deep as I look can I see, only as much as I dream can I be."

~ Karen Ravn

What's next? This question drives many of our daily activities, plenty of our decisions, and much of what we think about. As we sit in another boring lecture, our minds begin devising plans for after class. We patiently listen to our bosses talk about issues that need resolution, wondering when we will have a chance to say what we think. We go months and months biting our tongues until finally asking "So are we ever going to be more than just 'friends'?" Our natural tendency to look forward creates expectations. While most of us are willing to think about the past and are open to experiencing the present, the future holds our attention like nothing else. Everything seems to lie before us. Our careers, our relationships, and our lives are in such flux that we can feel compelled to think about how it will all turn out. This is not a new place to be for any group of young people, but how will our generation handle it? What's next for us?

Journey Back

It helps to understand where we have come from to understand what's next. Our journey began with this question: *Who am I?* With expectations surrounding us, the journey

presents obstacles at every turn. The people who tell us who
we should be, the Should-Bees, try to assign labels that are like
a blanket over something unseen and much deeper within us.
If we catch the Comparison Bug, what's under the blanket remains there as we follow trends that are not ours. All the
social outlets for expressing everything we think and feel are a
great way to let others know what's under the blanket, but in
themselves do not drive our process of digging deeper. It takes
something a little sturdier, with a bit more power. It's a piece
of equipment that's been sitting on our shoulders the entire
time: our minds.

Our minds enable us to be aware of the Should-Bees
and Comparison Bugs while we reflect on who we are apart
from the pressure of expectations. With reflection and active
questioning, we can reach one of our biggest goals: freedom.
We can use our new understanding to become free to be who
we really are. We can uncover the core personal values that
point to our purposes on earth. With our life agendas properly
prioritized, we have freedom to act according to our deepest
selves.

Freedom makes us feel like anything is possible and, as
history has shown, when we use our minds amazing things can
happen. We can change situations. But first we must understand our choices. Initially they may seem unlimited because
so many resources are available. However, our individual natures determine our decisions to use (or not use) the resources
available in a beneficial way. And the driving force behind

these decisions is our attitude, particularly passion. Passion can fuel us to overcome seemingly insurmountable challenges. To a great extent, we try to understand ourselves as individuals in order to figure out what we are passionate about. We want to know what makes life worth living.

Inevitably, we face tough situations that reveal our personal limitations and are difficult to overcome. We have no clue what these situations will be or when they will arrive. The uncertainty can be unsettling, so we search for ways to deal with it. We look to entertainment to distract us, to education and careers to guide us, to others for support, or to our deeper selves to steady us. If none of these deliver the stability we need, we may turn to faith. The life principles faith provides can help us reach our personal potential, see the true value of others, and feel secure in insecure situations. It can help us understand ourselves as individuals and inspire choices that mesh with our core values. However, it does not work unless we give it a try.

Our journeys would not have much significance if we were not trying to get somewhere. We constantly ask ourselves *Where am I going?* and *How am I getting there?* We have goals, but we will never accomplish them unless we do something to jump start us into action and ward off distractions. We need discipline to follow through with our plans. We need mindfulness to be aware of everything around us and remind us to appreciate our lives. Finally, we need the right attitude.

An attitude of optimism and urgency can propel us toward unimaginable places.

The people who cheer us on are people we feel connected to. Something about their cheers shows they needed us to accomplish what we did. They depend on us, as we depend on them for support. This state of interdependence helps us balance our desire for independence with our need for others. It reveals that everyone is like us in some aspects and helps us connect with others in a mutually beneficial way.

The journey of this book is based upon journeys taken before. Men and women have travelled similar roads with hopes of seeing a glimmer of progress in their lifetimes and of creating a better tomorrow for those who follow. People like W.E.B. Dubois, who sought to close the gap between oppressed minorities and the majority through education and empowerment of the disenfranchised. People like Winston Churchill, who used his military genius to defeat Adolph Hitler. People like Zhao Ziyang, who fought for the freedom of the people though it cost him his position in the Chinese government. People like Robert F. Kennedy, who emerged from the shadow of his brother, John F. Kennedy, to become a leader in his own right – a leader who fought to usher in a new type of America. His assertion that "Some men see things as they are and say why. I dream things that never were and say, why not." echoes in the ears of our generation.

Then there were individuals whose actions were so powerful they spurred men and women across cities, states, and nations to action. People like Dolores Huerta, who cofounded the Agriculture Workers Association and organized people to fight for fair wages for farm workers. People like Che Guevara, whose rebellion against tyrants for the sake of the masses and uncompromising pursuit of his ideals led to a revolution in Latin America that is still imprinted in our collective conscious. People like Rosa Parks, whose decision to stay seated began the civil rights movement. Her decision continues to reverberate in the fabric of our society. These people paved the road for our journeys.

Dawn

One of the most magnificent life experiences is witnessing a sunrise. I once saw this majestic event from a balcony that overlooked a gorgeous beach. The air that filled the late moments of the night and the early moments of the morning held a refreshing crispness. The stillness was only disrupted by the rhythmic sound of my breathing. As the rays of sunlight peeked over the horizon, the sky awakened and began to resemble an artist's canvas gently decorated in lavender and magenta. Birds chirped and a soothing, cool breeze emanated from the ocean. Despite my fatigue, my eyes could not turn away from the stunning sight before me: the dawn of a new day.

The dawn of a new generation represents an equally magnificent display of splendor. Before reaching young adulthood, we had much to learn. As children, our parents and other adults in our lives taught us how to behave in public, care for ourselves, and think about how the world works. In our preteen years, we looked to our friends to learn about friendship and what was cool. Our teenage years helped us learn about ourselves, our goals in life, and love. While each experience made us the people we are today, it was difficult to have an objective perspective then. We lacked the maturity to make sense of the arguments with parents, the pain of a breakup, and the push to achieve. We were not developed enough to see the significance of our life experiences and the magnitude of our potential.

With these experiences behind us and the future ahead, the beginning of something special is brewing. We are awakening to the possibilities our lives hold, both as individuals and as a generation. We are beginning to grasp the depth of our personal and collective potential. We understand that the human capacity to adapt in order to overcome challenges is strengthened by our technological savvy and ambition. We are coming of age when the world is in dire need. We stand perfectly poised to use our experiences to fuel our dreams. At the dawn of this new day, our generation's awakening is the spark that can make the rest of the day meaningful.

Movement

Waking up in the morning is possibly the most difficult task known to mankind. The mere sound of the alarm clock signals the end of a restful night and an eventual exit from a warm and comfortable bed. It really is torture. I would immediately and automatically eliminate the buzz of the alarm by hitting the top of my clock. The problem with this strategy was that it delayed the start to my day and produced sly attempts to sneak into the back of classes unnoticed (hard for a six-foot guy wearing Daffy Duck™ pajamas). After a few too many mean stares from my professors, I decided to move the alarm clock far away from my bed. I had to get up to turn it off. The first couple of days were annoying because I kept reaching to turn off a nonexistent alarm beside my bed, forgetting I had to get up and walk over to it. After the first week I finally got used to the routine and actually felt more awake in the morn-ing because of it. I realized that the only way to awaken fully is through movement.

As our generation fully awakens to its potential, the world waits to see if movement will follow. The actions of men and women before us defined their generations and laid the foundation for the world we live in today. Many used rallies, protests, sit-ins, demonstrations to create this world. These were their movements.

What is our generation's movement? The first logical step is to figure out *where* to move. Do we take on the chal-lenges of past generations? Can we really build the homes, communities, nations, and world that the great men and wom-en before us envisioned? Do we have what it takes to make Dr. King's dream a reality, or to move closer to the type of service to one another John F. Kennedy asked us to have? Not only do the old threats to the world persist, but we face new challenges.

At the start of the twenty-first century, *Time* magazine published a series of special editions that reflected on the twentieth century and imagined the century to come. The conclusion of most of the scholars, writers, and leaders of the past century who weighed in was that despite significant progress in the twentieth century, the challenges for the twenty-first century were quickly mounting. Global climate change that threatens quality of life, ideological fundamentalism that has the potential to spark a nuclear war, and a world economy that is potentially crippled by a downturn in one country are just a few of the minefields our generation has to navigate. Each of these challenges is more than overwhelming for any generation, but to pile them onto the residual challenges inherited from the past seems insurmountable. Do we have the tools? Are we as a generation capable of becoming who we need to be in order to face and conquer these difficult situations?

From the start, it was clear that technology made our generation unique. Computers, video game systems, and the Internet were not things we discovered during our teenage years or additions to the world we already knew as adults. We got these gadgets as soon as we left the crib. With them, we learned about life issues and had exposure to situations earlier in life than our parents ever imagined. We grew up in an interconnected and increasingly integrated world of innovation and technology that overcomes limitations from just a few decades ago. This "new world" of technology and cyberspace is all we ever knew. In essence, we are the first generation to know the global village as our only home.

By the time we entered grade school, the question *Why?* was as familiar to us as the cyberworld. We were taught from the beginning to question everything. Whether it was explicitly conveyed by our parents telling us "Think before you act" or implicitly learned when a kid on television disobeyed rules that did not make sense, our inquisitive minds asked *Why?* rather than blindly follow. Unlike the rebellious, confrontational *Why?* that characterized the 1960s, for example, our *Why?* was more inquisitive. We wanted our actions to make sense. We needed to know that every bit of effort we extended to follow a rule, meet others' expectations, or accomplish a small personal goal was worth the time and energy. This was reinforced in school as we were told to think critically about situations and "facts" we learned. We were taught never to take information at face value, but instead to do everything possible to understand it. With our seemingly limitless access to information, we would look anything up online and figure it out immediately. Our generation does not simply *want* to know but *needs* to know *Why?*

As young adults, we are still trying to make sense of all of these experiences while thinking about the future. In many ways, we stand at a crossroad. While the choices for where to move next can appear overwhelming, moving toward one another while appreciating and contributing to our unique individuality seems foundational.

After figuring out *where* to move, we need to figure out *how* to move. How can we pave the road for future generations? What tools do we have at our disposal? In their ingenious book *Freakonomics*, Steven Levitt and Stephen Dubner argue that a significant shift in recent decades has fundamentally changed the way we do business. Rather than "ask the expert," as previous generations did, we have the tool our generation knows best: the Internet. Because we can gather information about the baseline price of a car or the cost of a medical procedure, for example, the experts no longer have the same power to control information and prices. The information age has given consumers access to expert information and therefore the marketplace. The power has shifted.

We are the first generation to understand the extent to which the Internet can provide information for us to progress personally and collectively. We know its potential to connect people and ideas. When coupled with our inquisitiveness about the complexity of the human experience, it is clear that our generation can use the shift in power produced by the Internet to move things forward. In one of his final conversations with his nephew, Uncle Ben turns to Peter and says, "With great power comes great responsibility." Peter Parker does not realize the relevance of these words as he begins his journey toward becoming Spiderman. With our great power, what is our great responsibility?

The questions of *where* and *how* movement happens pale in comparison to one final question: *what* will happen

when this road is paved? With each step forward, our movement paves a road that those who follow must walk, while also
building our legacy. We were raised in a world that preaches
understanding and appreciation of the complexity and diversity of the human experience. How can we use our power to take
on the responsibility inherent in these words and put it into
action? We have already begun to answer this question with
our knack for exposing corruption and actions that threaten us
individually and collectively. We tape an abuse of human
rights and put it on YouTube™ for the world to see, with hopes
that someone will view this inhumanity and take corrective
action. We e-mail, text, tweet, and blog about the issues that
concern us and that we believe need change. We collect dona-
tions and signatures for petitions online so that we can present
our concerns to political leaders and make them accountable
for their actions.

What more will we do? Will we make greater efforts to
disseminate accurate information about people? Are we willing to have the tough, honest conversations in public that we
have in our inner circles? Will we create new opportunities for
those who are disenfranchised? Will we face the global challenges ahead with a concern for all humanity or succumb to
fear and only ensure our own protection and prosperity? Will
we do more?

While the legacy of our generation is unknown, we and
older generations agree that there is no shortage of high expectations among us. Yet, these expectations are often assailed as

nice dreams that will soon meet "reality." We are described as wanting too much too soon, or wanting too much for too little. Observing us at work, at home, and in our social circles, our refusal to lower expectations often befuddles older people. We want the rights and privileges of our parents. We believe we deserve certain luxuries that our parents have, even as we have not been around as long. We see the world as we want it to be; our parents say they see it as it is. To them, we still appear asleep. Our lives do not seem radical enough. Our actions do not appear urgent enough. Our vision does not look clear enough.

In *The First World War*, military historian John Keegan describes in gripping detail how the British lost 70,000 troops in a battle during World War I. Before this devastating loss, the British Empire was nearly unmatched, largely because of its belief in its strength and dominance for the future. After this massive loss of life, a pivotal loss of vital optimism occurred. *Vital optimism* is the fundamental belief that the best days are yet to come, no matter the circumstances. It is this vital optimism, Keegan argues, that is often the lifeblood that propels nations forward.

Some find it hard to believe that our generation will embark upon a movement. For those who do believe, it may be difficult to see how we will go about it. The Internet, the social networks, and the new ways we think about the human experience and express our individuality seem so elusive that it's hard to pinpoint how we will come together to move the

132

world forward. Some say that our generation is too idealistic, that we are naïve, that we want too much, and that our expectations are too high. They do not seem to see that beneath the cool exterior that exudes confidence lie hopes and dreams for the future, the discipline and resourcefulness to overcome any obstacle, and the passion to push past anyone who dares stand in the way. What many fail to realize is that our generation simply understands the best is yet to come.

Postlude:
Beautiful

Isn't it beautiful?
I am awakened by the smile of sunshine,
And the breeze that gently grazes my face.
Regardless of the conditions around me,
It is amazing to just take that breath and wake.
Plus, I get to wake up to this ...
A world that is diverse in every possible way.
From the people who inhabit it
To the myriad of emotions I can feel each day.
The morning ritual of getting ready
Sometimes feels routine and boring,
But I am grateful to have somewhere to go
Each and every morning.

The day continues to steadily move forward.
I feel the stress of being at the job late
And the burden of having schoolwork to complete.
Yet, I'm always reminded of those who cheer me along the
way.
The memories of family that encourage me to move forward,
The conversations with friends by cell, e-mail, or text
Help me still feel deeply connected to the world
While also reminding me to press towards what's next.

At some point, the ups and downs always come.
Like the joys of being in love
Or the pain of being out of it
Often compel me to look above.
I search for answers that I know I may not find,
But doesn't this make the human experience unique?
An experience full of mysteries involving both triumph and
tragedy,
A journey that can potentially bring our passions to peak.
The bruises and bumps that have gotten me here
Or the disastrous events that can happen to a nation,
Have a funny way of showing me that nothing is lost

But instead death is an opportunity for new life's reincarnation.

Life's offerings sometimes overwhelm me.
It seems too amazing and too sad all at the same time.
The triumph and tragedy that eventually touch us all
Permit me to see the beauty that lies behind.
With all that life has to offer,
It makes it very difficult to watch from the sideline.
Because experiencing every moment is experiencing
The beauty that is life ... the beauty that is mine.
Isn't it beautiful?

Reader's Guide

About This Reader's Guide

Congratulations for deciding to read this book and think about some interesting, and sometimes tough, issues Generation Why is facing. The chapters and their interludes each explore a central topic from a variety of perspectives, including historical context, current societal trends, and Generation Why itself. Given the breadth of the exploration, it made sense to provide a Reader's Guide.

The purpose of the Reader's Guide is to create opportunities to expand on the ideas discussed in the book through group discussion and personal reflection. Its questions and activities are for small groups interested in sparking further discussion, teachers interested in hands-on activities and discussion for class assignments, and individuals wishing to reflect more deeply.

The Reader's Guide is divided into six parts, which mirror the chapters and interludes. Each segment includes:

- **Discussion questions** to spark conversation within small groups. Questions are written in an open-ended format so participants can explain the reason for their answers.
- Three **reflection scenarios** to encourage deeper personal reflection about a topic. These may provide the basis for an essay, blog post, personal journal entry, or further group discussion.

- Two **activities** that provide hands-on opportunities to explore the questions raised in chapters. These activities also may provide the basis for interesting group discussion.

For more information about *The Dawn of Generation Why* and additional resources, please visit www.GenerationWhyMovement.org.

Enjoy the book and have a great personal journey!

Chapter 1:
Who Are You?

Discussion Questions

- How do others try to influence your perception of yourself?
- Who are some of the Should-Bees in your life?
- What types of comparisons are most frustrating to you? Why?
- How do you deal with Should-Bees and Comparison Bugs?
- Have social networking tools changed the way you describe yourself?
- Would you describe yourself as a Nonstopper, Whatever, Know, or a combination?
- What was the last personal belief you challenged? What did you learn from challenging this belief?
- What are the top three items on your life agenda?

Reflection Scenarios

It is sixty years from today and you are sitting around the dinner table with your children, grandchildren, and great-grandchildren. One of your teenage grandchildren asks you what it was like when you were growing up. Your grandchildren want you to describe what was important to people your age as young adults. They wonder what your generation wanted to be when they grew up. They want to know what the trends and pop culture were like. They want to know what the biggest influences on you were as a young adult. What would you tell your children and grandchildren?

Describe yourself using only five adjectives. Which would you choose? Why those? Now think about whether these are the same five adjectives you would have chosen to describe yourself five years ago. What has changed and what is similar? Finally, what changes or similarities do you anticipate for the next five years? Why?

Imagine you are diagnosed with a rare form of brain cancer and will live only six more months. What would the top five items on your life agenda be? Why? How would you achieve these goals in the next six months?

Activities

Identify an issue in which your position differs significantly from the Should-Bees around you. Write a letter to one of these Should-Bees that explains your position and tells the Should-Bee that the relationship is important to you and you want to preserve it.

Write a one-paragraph biography of yourself explaining what makes you unique and how this relates to your purpose in life.

Chapter 2:
Choice

Discussion Questions

- What was the last big challenge you faced? Did you overcome it? How?
- Do we have a choice in every situation or are we sometimes without choices?
- What resources do you have available to overcome obstacles?
- What is one personal skill that you want to significantly improve?
- How would you describe your attitude? How do you think it influence your experiences?
- How does a person find and maintain a passion in life?

Reflection Scenarios

Think back to an obstacle in your life that seemed insurmountable, but that you did overcome by using your mind to come up with creative strategies. Could you apply these strategies to an obstacle in your life that you have not yet overcome?

Think of a skill that you want to improve. Now imagine yourself at twelve years old. What would you advise your twelve-year-old self to do in order to develop this skill? Who would you suggest talking with? What resources would you recommend? Can your responses help you start improving this skill today?

Imagine you were involved in an accident that left you deaf and blind. How would you respond? How would you feel? Who would you contact for comfort? Now imagine yourself twelve months later. What do you think your attitude would be? What resources would you have used to adapt? Finally, imagine that your hearing and sight were restored five years after the accident occurred. What opportunities would you then have? What do you think your attitude would be? What about your self-image? What do you think you would have learned from the accident and its aftermath?

Activities

Think about a choice or decision that you've delayed making. Divide and label a sheet of paper like this:

Making the Decision	Not Making the Decision
Pros	Pros
Cons	Cons

Fill in the worksheet. Then turn the paper over and note:

- your deadline for making this decision
- the names of two people whose advice you value who you will consult
- the reward you'll give yourself after the decision is made

Put this worksheet where you'll see it every day, and follow through on the commitment you've made to yourself (and the reward).

Choose a person you find very passionate about life. Find or take a picture of this person and tape it onto a sheet of paper. Below the image, you're going to create a caption to describe your "real-life superhero." What makes this person your real-life superhero? What does he or she do that shows passion? What is his or her attitude? Who does this person generally surround him- or herself with? How does he or she use the resources available to him/her? Place this picture in a visible place that will remind you of these qualities you admire on a daily basis.

Chapter 3:
Faith

Discussion Questions

- Is faith relevant to you?
- Do you believe that science can potentially replace faith? Are faith and science mutually exclusive?
- Do you think faith deserves more discussion in public forums, such as schools?
- Do the life principles of faith have the potential to inspire you to become better?
- Can you think of an example of people using religion to hurt or divide others?
- Can you think of an example of people using faith to help others or create unity?
- Can an atheist have and benefit from faith?
- How can people who adhere to different faith traditions have an open conversation about faith?

Reflection Scenarios

You are a top consultant at the most prestigious consulting firm in your field. For your most recent assignment, your boss wants you to advise the client to take a course of action that will significantly hurt the client's company but that can easily be blamed on poor implementation by the client. Your boss's thinking is that this will cause the client to return to your firm to "fix" the "problems." Will you disobey direction by providing the consultation that you know is best for your client (and risk your job) or follow orders? What values will inform your decision? Would faith play a role? After you make your decision, how will you live with it?

Think back to a difficult time in your life, when the situation appeared bleak. How did you endure? Did anything or anyone sustain you? If so, who or what was it? Was this resource one you relied on before and can rely on again? If not, can you imagine anything or anyone that could provide you with a secure base?

You've been bitten by a snake while on a hike with friends on a vacation overseas. Your friends take a picture of the snake and google it while trying to contact the forest ranger. They learn the snake was poisonous and without an antidote you will die in an hour. What thoughts do you think would cross your mind? After the ranger arrives with the antidote and you are saved, do you think any of your life priorities would have changed? If so, how?

Activities

You are a journalist with an assignment to write a feature on the past, present, and future of faith. Your editor wants you to take a generational, multi-perspective approach. The first generation is your parents'. How did faith influence their style of parenting and the household you grew up in? The second generation is yours. What role does faith play in Gen Y-ers' relationships and careers? What role might it play? Last, your editor wants you to look at the next generation and the role faith might play. What resources will you use to research and write this feature? Once you have the information, write the article.

A scientist has invented specialized technology that transmits matter into the farthest reaches of space, and it is now possible to send a letter to God. In a worldwide contest, you were selected to write the letter. Its content will be between you and God. What would you write?

Chapter 4:
Goals: A Work in Progress

Discussion Questions

- What is the *Why?* or passion that drives you?
- How do you define success?
- What prevents you from taking action when you've been inspired by a goal?
- How do you deal with distractions?
- Is your perspective about what is necessary to achieve goals realistic? Why or why not?
- How do you stay committed to your goal when you are halfway there?
- How might you create and maintain discipline while working toward a goal?
- Do you think there's a relationship between mindfulness and passion when it comes to reaching a goal?
- What strategies might you adopt to maintain the "right" attitude toward a goal?

Reflection Scenarios

You are on a racecourse and the finish line is a goal you want to achieve. Several fallen logs cross the path, making the course difficult to run. Each log is a distraction from your goal. Why are the logs there? Can they serve any positive purpose? Write down the distraction each log represents, and a strategy for getting around it to the finish line.

What is one goal you've had over the past year but have not worked toward? What were the major obstacles? Who could help? Make a plan for achieving the goal that includes seeking the advice of two people and two strategies for countering each obstacle. Set a deadline for creating the plan. Once you have a plan, ask a trusted person to check with you on a regular basis (perhaps once a week) to see if you are following through.

Imagine yourself twenty years from now as a successful person. What does that mean to you? What is your career, if any? What do you spend most of your time doing? Who are the people in your life? Where do you live? Then think about what you are doing to become this successful person. What do you need to do today to move toward this goal? This year? Five years from now? Ten?

Activities

To practice mindfulness, find a quiet place to sit and close your eyes. Focus all your attention on one part of your body and try to notice all the sensations that arise. Then move your attention slowly to other body parts. After a few minutes, focus on your breathing. Try to let all the thoughts running through your head go and focus on your body as you breathe. After a few minutes, open your eyes. How did this exercise feel? Would using this exercise during the day help keep your attention on the present moment and appreciate your surroundings? How?

Identify a goal you want to accomplish and write it on the top of a sheet of paper. Below the goal, outline a plan for achieving it. Then divide the sheet of paper so it looks like the example on the next page.

Under Do, make notes for keeping the right attitude, mindset, and discipline for implementing your plan and achieving your goal. Under Don't, caution yourself against possible obstacles in each category.

At the bottom, give yourself a deadline. Place this worksheet in a visible place, and do it!

Goal:

Plan:

	Do	Don't
Attitude		
Mindset		
Discipline		

Deadline:

Chapter 5:
Interdependence

Discussion Questions

- How do you use technology to connect with others?
- Does technology affect the quality of communication between you and others?
- Have the major differences between our generation's style of connecting and older generation's style impacted you at your job? If so, how?
- What obstacles still exist to connecting with others? How do we overcome them?
- How have globalization and the quick exchange of information influenced how you define connection?
- What are strategies for appreciating the uniqueness of others while also acknowledging human commonality?
- Do your interactions with others affect your personal satisfaction? If so, how? If not, why not?
- Do you face any obstacles to achieving a personal balance between dependence and independence? If so, what are they?
- Do you connect with others in an interdependent manner? How?
- How has social networking impacted your friendships and/or romantic relationships?

Reflection Scenarios

A time machine has sent you seventy-five years in the past and to one of the most populated cities in the country. What kinds of prejudice do you think you'd observe? How would you react? If you were to meet your grandparents as young adults during your time travel, how would you describe the social atmosphere seventy-five years in the future? What accomplishments would you note? What obstacles to further social progress would you identify?

Consider the most recent major natural disaster you heard about. What thoughts crossed your mind? Did you feel connected or disconnected to the victims? To what extent did your connection to the victims affect your reactions? Would your reaction have been different if your level of connection was different? How?

You were left on an island with a band of thieves, no belongings or electronic devices, and an unstable bridge as the only way off the island to safety. You are suspicious of the group, but need help to cross the bridge. If you reach the other side safely, will you look at this group of people differently? How? Does this scenario have any parallels in your everyday life?

Activities

Research a neighborhood near where you live that you've never visited. Use the Internet and library books to identify historical landmarks, change (or lack of change) in demographics, and qualities of the neighborhood and its inhabitants. What are the common challenges the people in that community face? Look for a community organization and volunteer for a project. How is this community different from yours? In what ways is it like yours? What direct or indirect impact do the people within this community have on you?

For one day, document at least ten contacts you have with others. They can be brief and casual contacts, or longer engagements. Take notes on each person, including gender, race, and economic status, and on the interaction itself. What effect did the interaction have on your sense of personal balance? Then write down how this person has the *potential* to affect you. Consider the potential financial, emotional, social, and personal impact and the effects they might have on your state of balance.

Chapter 6:
Steps

Discussion Questions

- What accomplishments from previous generations do you think have had the biggest impact on our generation?
- What are ways that people can awaken in order to understand more about themselves personally?
- How is our generation perceived by older generations?
- How would you describe our generation to future generations?
- What influence is our generation having on future generations?
- What are the biggest challenges facing our generation over the next ten years? What are some strategies for dealing with these challenges?
- How can technology help us create a better future?
- What personal characteristics does our generation need to contribute positively to the world over the next twenty-five years?
- What role does globalization play in your life?
- What aspect of being a young adult today are you most appreciative of?

Reflection Scenarios

Imagine yourself as a young adult 75 years from now in the same town you live in. What changes might you expect to see? Are people more or less connected with one another? What is the economy like? What impact did Generation Y have? What one piece of advice would you give to the young adults of the future?

Fifteen years from now, you are an academic counselor for college students. Based on your experiences as a young adult, what advice would you give students? What suggestions would you give this student that are of personal use to you now?

You are approaching your one hundredth birthday and your family is having a big party for you. They've asked that you share stories about your young adulthood at the party. They're curious about your generation, about what you most appreciate about those times, and about how the challenges and triumphs of that era molded you. They're also curious if you have any regrets and what you'd change if you had a chance. What would you say? Could anything you would say help you make better decisions now?

Activities

You've been asked to create a time capsule with ten items that characterize you and your generation. The capsule will be opened in 100 years. What five items would you include that characterize you personally? What five items that characterize our generation? Why these items? What do they suggest our generation's legacy will be? If you had to choose the one item that best characterizes you and represents the legacy you would like to leave, which would it be? What can you put in motion today to make sure this becomes your legacy? If you keep that item where you can see it every day, it could help you build that legacy.

A popular tour company has asked you to design a brochure for a tour of our generation. Where are the top five places you would suggest people visit? What are the top five activities? Whose names would you mention? Why?

Bibliography

Introduction

Armour, S. (2005, November 6). Generation Y: They've arrived at work with a new attitude. *USA Today.* Retrieved June 9, 2009, from http://www.usatoday.com/money/workplace/2005-11-06-gen-y_x.htm

Generation Y. (1993, August 30). *Advertising Age*, 16.

Strauss, W., & Howe, N. (1992). *Generations: The history of America's future, 1584 to 2069*. New York: Harper Perennial.

Twenge, J.M. (2006). *Generation Me: Why today's young Americans are more confident, assertive, entitled - And more miserable than ever before.* New York: Free Press.

Chapter 1

Ellison, R. (1995). *Invisible man.* New York: Random House.

Palahniuk, C. (1996). *Fight club: A novel.* New York: Henry Holt.

Twenge, J.M. (2006). *Generation Me: Why today's young Americans are more confident, assertive, entitled - And more miserable than ever before.* New York: Free Press.

Chapter 2

Essays, philosophical and psychological. (1908). In honor of William James, professor in Harvard University, by his colleagues at Columbia University. Cambridge: University Press.

Frankl, V.E. (2006). *Man's search for meaning.* Boston: Beacon Press.

Hill, N. (2005). *Think and grow rich: The landmark bestseller – Now revised and updated for the 21st century* (rev. ed.). New York: Tarcher/Penguin.

Mandela, N. (1995). *Long walk to freedom: The autobiography of Nelson Mandela.* Boston: Back Bay Books.

Chapter 3

Collins, F. S. (2006). *The language of God: A scientist presents evidence for belief.* New York: Free Press.

Gandhi, M. (1993). *Gandhi: An autobiography: The story of my experiments with truth.* Boston: Beacon Press.

King, Jr., M. L. (2001). *The autobiography of Martin Luther King, Jr.* (C. Carson, Ed.) New York: Warner Books.

Kluger, J. (2009, February 12). The biology of belief. *Time.* Retrieved July 2, 2010, from http://www.time.com/time/health/article/0,8599,1879016,00.html

Strobel, L. (2000). *The case for faith*: *A journalist investigates the toughest objections to Christianity.* Grand Rapids, MI: Zondervan.

Chapter 4

Colvin, G. (2006, October 19). What it takes to be great. *Fortune.* Retrieved April 13, 2009, from http://money.cnn.com/magazines/fortune/fortune_archive/2006/10/30/8391794/index.htm

Gladwell, M. (2002). *The tipping point*: *How little things can make a big difference.* Boston: Back Bay Books.

Kabat-Zinn, J. (2006). *Mindfulness for beginners* [Audiobook]. Louisville, CO: Sounds True.

Tolle, E. (2005). *A new earth: Awakening to your life's purpose.* New York: Penguin.

Chapter 5

Aronson, E. (1990). Applying social psychology to desegregation and energy conservation. *Personality and Social Psychology Bulletin,* 16, 118-132.

Jung, C., & Storr, A. (1983). *The essential Jung.* Princeton, NJ: Princeton University Press.

McLuhan, M. (1962). *The Gutenberg galaxy: The making of typographic man.* Toronto: University of Toronto Press.

Chapter 6

Keegan, J. (2000). *The first world war*. New York: Vintage Books.

Levitt, S., & Dubner, S. (2005). *Freakonomics: A rogue economist explores the hidden side of everything.* New York: HarperCollins.

Ramo, J.C. (1998, April 13). The shape of the future. *Time*. Retrieved June 3, 2009, from http://205.188.238.109/time/time100/leaders/future/future.html

About the Author

Born and raised in Washington D.C., Isaiah B. Pickens attended George Washington University. His college experiences ranged from student government to athletics, and created the desire to explore the issues most relevant to young adults and pursue a career in psychology. Pickens is currently a graduate student in clinical psychology at Fordham University. He plans to continue developing stories that are relevant to the lives of young people. He is the founder of iOPENING ENTERPRISES, a creative arts firm, and Generation Why Movement, a nonprofit organization geared toward providing self-improvement and community engagement resources to young adults between the ages of 18 and 29. He resides in New York City.

6396442R0

Made in the USA
Lexington, KY
16 August 2010